MODERN ATTACHMENT PARENTING

MODERN ATTACHMENT PARENTING

The Comprehensive Guide to Raising a Secure Child

JAMIE GRUMET

Foreword by Alanis Morissette

Introduction by William Sears, MD

ROCKRIDGE
PRESS

Cover Design: Erin Wengrovius & Matt Girard

Interior Design: Matt Girard

Art Producer: Sue Bischofberger

Editor: Morgan Shanahan

Production Editor: Mia Moran

Illustrations © Erin Wengrovius, 2019

ISBN: Print 978-1-64611-036-0 | eBook 978-1-64611-037-7

R0

To Samuel and Aram,
the true joy and loves of my life.
I have stumbled so many times as your mother, and I am sure I will
stumble, even fail you, countless more.
Thank you for lifting me up and allowing me to learn, grow,
and share my mistakes with others.
I am enough.

And I will never be enough.

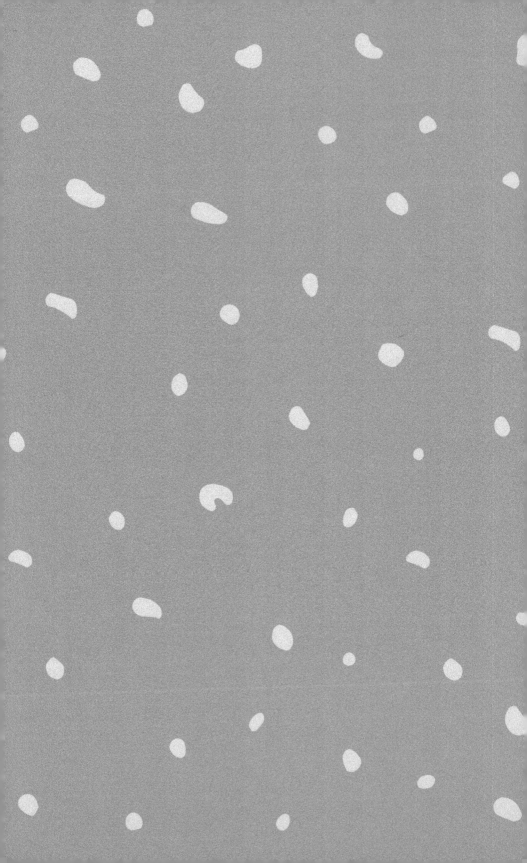

Contents

Foreword

In 2012 I saw Jamie Grumet on the cover of *Time* magazine nursing her son. There she stood: brazen, intelligent, courageous, and, I guessed, in the middle of what might be a hailstorm of reactions and unsolicited feedback. My assumption was that this "feedback" might have been passionate...some excited about her standing there, unapologetic about nursing her son who was still benefiting from this scientifically and anthropologically proven form of connection and nurturance with her. I also assumed the feedback might be filled with rejection and upset—at worst cruel and uninformed and potentially violent in its veracity toward her. I also wanted to let out a yelp for how exciting it was that the idea of being "mom enough" was being discussed publicly in such a forum. That this archetypal role of mother was being put on the table to be openly dissected, along with all that comes with it: The pressure. The beauty. The overwhelm. The maternal fire. The heavy burden of perfectionism. The tenderness. The activism. The unnaturalness of it happening without a village in modern society. I was lit up at the thought that Jamie, with her son Aram would become a symbol... and somehow incite a more active conversation in our culture. A far-reaching conversation on psychosocial and macro levels. To me, this photo on this cover was connoting a step forward in feminism, emboldening an empathy toward the life-giving mother, and I dare say, a nice little jump in the evolution in consciousness itself (no pressure Jamie—ha) as it seemed willing to peek under the hood of what "parenting well enough" even means in our current times. To me, this cover had the potential to shine the light on how attachment is the underpinned movement that dictates what kind of culture and society we create as human beings as a whole. No small role Jamie volunteered to play.

I reached out to her immediately and had the privilege of going to lunch with her shortly thereafter. I wanted to support her, empathize with what I was assuming was a storm-of-a-time for her, and have a rich conversation with someone who was thoughtful and equally passionate about one of my favorite subjects: Attachment.

And more specifically, attachment parenting. You can imagine our lunch—a lot of parity and laughing and geeking out and diving deeply into the anthropology, science, physiology, psychology, and developmental effects of the bond of attachment parenting, and all that it yields in our children-grown-into-adults.

So much of the time, we don't see the full effects of our parenting until our children grow into adulthood, although we certainly have glimpses. And yes, while nature cannot be shifted, the nurture aspect IS on us. As heady and as daunting and exciting and exhausting as that is—it truly is up to us to nail (as best as we can) the "nurture" part. This book is a huge help in that regard. A godsend to those of us who want to know how to approach attachment in our families in such a way that honors our day to day hours and values and considerations that are unique to our way of living.

The perhaps counter-intuitive aspect of attachment parenting is that the more closeness and responsivity and attunement and secure connection a child receives in their early years...the more grounded they feel as they venture out. And the likelier they are to live an authentic and self-expressed and contributing life. With a securely attached person...there is a higher chance that they will move out into the world trusting life, trusting themselves, trusting that love and mutuality is possible...and trusting that they are worthy enough to receive tenderness as well as offer it, and that they can trust themselves enough to be discerning as they navigate around in their relationships. This is the great payoff and effect of our attachments being secure early on in life. This security goes beyond the intellect and anchors itself beyond cognition...into the fibers of our bodies. And I would say keeps the light on in our souls.

The good news: Healing and corrective experience can shift things if our caregivers (or we as caregivers) didn't provide secure attachment. Neuroplasticity and safe-enough relationships can help heal and resolve any ruptures we experienced, later in life. Thank god for that. It does take some of what could be a self-punishment for "getting at this information too late" and softens the blow. Yet wouldn't it be great if all the energy it took to correct our traumas and sense of disconnection could be spent elsewhere? Wouldn't it be ideal if we could provide this, as best as we can, so that our children can keep their energy focused on serving their loved ones, their community, and the world at large? Would there, also, not be some element of healing for our very own selves, and our own attachment wounds, in the offering of this attuned kind of love to our children?

This book is a bridge of a kind—an important one—that is beginning to more formally link attachment theory—the theory started by John Bowlby and Mary Ainsworth, and expanded upon by leading thinkers of our time Sue Johnson, Diane Poole Heller, Allan Schore, Dan Siegel, and many more. It also touches on the earliest of the stages of development itself—theories originated and expanded upon by Piaget, Erik Erikson, Sabrina Spielrein, John Bradshaw, Margaret Mahler, Harville Hendrix, and Gordon Neufeld, among others. This book effortlessly and conversationally touches into how attachment parenting has been ever-present in different cultures around the planet. And most importantly—it shows in very direct, utterly readable and tangible ways how we can apply this understanding into our modern lives. There are as many different approaches to parenting as there are families in this world, all of us with different takes on "how to do this thing called parenting." Depending upon your reasons for reading this book: Whether it be to inform you for the first time, inspire you in tiny or big ways, affirm what you already know, or usher you toward a path that felt intuitively right but you never had support around you to pursue—may this book serve as a treasure trove of inspiration and application, both. There is so much validating, comforting and enlightening information in this book. May it support you on your path of care that you uniquely offer in your life....and may it thank you for the care it took to pick this book up to begin with. Because this care...for your children, for your family, for their development, for their security...just might contribute to healing and abating all that ails us in this society we live in.

- Alanis Morissette, Writer, Artist, Activist

P.S. I wrote parts of this while nursing, and then pumping. Thanks, Jamie :)

Introduction

When Martha and I first worked out the principles of attachment parenting, published in 1992 in *The Baby Book*, our effort was touted as a new theory on parenting. The style of parenting we described (from observing, beginning in the early '70s, families in my pediatric practice whose children were thriving) boils down to one thing: doing what feels natural for parents and baby. This concept is something that families all over the world have done intuitively, long before there was a book industry or the luxury of choosing one's parenting style.

Naturally, what worked for Martha and I as we raised our own children—and as we have supported our adult children and the parents in my practice and those reading our books—has also developed over the years as the parenting landscape has been shifting. As you will read in *Modern Attachment Parenting*, Jamie Grumet has had a pivotal role in the resurgence of the attachment parenting conversation, brought about by her appearance on the May 21, 2012 cover of *Time* magazine.

My role in the spread of attachment parenting was the cover story that week (timed apparently to come out on Mother's Day) because it had been 20 years since *The Baby Book* had been published. The headline on the cover, "Are You Mom Enough?" caught us and everyone by surprise. It seemed to pose a challenge: If you aren't breastfeeding, and if you are not breastfeeding a child well past toddlerhood, are you really mom enough? Each mom reading that headline and the story itself had to consider that question. It was our firm opinion that each and every one of those moms would be saying a resounding YES, of course, I am mom enough!

It was Jamie's confidence as a mom that was captured in that cover photo and she will tell you that story herself in this book. Her story and her contribution to the ongoing discussion of how to navigate the waters of parenting has been a blessing for the AP community and incidentally also for our family. As we've gotten to know Jamie, and as we have watched a steady stream of new parents coming through my pediatric practice, we've gotten to know and appreciate this new breed of attachment parent. This is a generation of loving and attentive parents with a unique set of challenges presented by the pace of modern life, having an equally strong desire to intimately understand their children and appropriately encourage and discipline them as they grow up, just as my wife and I did.

I'm thrilled to have had a hand in introducing Jamie Grumet to the world and I look forward to seeing the ways she continues to show her generation of parents how AP can work for and strengthen their unique families. Welcome to parenting intuitively. As Jamie says, "You're already great at it!"

- William Sears, MD, Coauthor of *The Baby Book* and *The Attachment Parenting Book*

Welcome to Intuitive Parenting: Yes, You Can Totally Do This

My name is Jamie Grumet, and I invite you to walk with me on the path of attachment parenting.

Becoming a parent is one of life's most incredible experiences. It's also natural, instinctive, beautiful, and transformative. Why, then, do parents resist their intuition and follow parenting "rules" that don't feel authentic?

Maybe we place so much stock in how we were raised that we believe the way our parents raised us is the only way. Perhaps society—or even just an overbearing relative—makes us feel that the parenting ideas we have are wrong, in contradiction to religious or social norms, or even dangerous. Maybe we constantly compare ourselves to other parents and wonder if we should do what they're doing instead. Maybe we just lack the confidence to listen to our gut.

You may be familiar with attachment parenting, but what you've learned might have been a little skewed or sensationalized by the media. I'd like to share what evolution has created and what science has learned about the seven Baby B's of attachment parenting, as coined by Dr. William Sears, renowned pediatrician and author of the bestseller *The Baby Book*.

As a parent, I strive to adhere to the road map for healthy attachment that Dr. Sears carefully laid out. As a human, I've found that adherence has not always been possible. My life doesn't look like the 1950s archetype of the nuclear family described in so many books on attachment parenting. Statistically speaking, yours doesn't either, which is why I wanted to create this book—to address each of the key tenets of attachment parenting and to offer suggestions for modifying these principles for your unique family structure or circumstance. If the modifications I offer still don't quite fit your family, that's okay, too. There's no one way to do this thing.

Both of my children had unique beginnings that don't align with popular notions of what attachment parenting looks like. Some of the Baby B's that we couldn't do when our sons were newborns included birth bonding, babywearing, and breastfeeding. With both boys, we integrated what worked for our family, and more became possible with time.

SECOND-GENERATION ATTACHMENT PARENT

My experience with attachment parenting began with my parents' decision to parent me according to my needs rather than society's wants. There was no name for this style of parenting; it was completely intuitive for my parents. My parents' approach came on the heels of their regret over the parenting choices they made with my older siblings.

My sister and brother were both conventionally parented in the 1970s. My sister seemed to fare well with this parenting style, but my brother did not. My mother said she knew she was parenting incorrectly for his needs, but because she was so worried about how other people viewed her, she fought all of her natural instincts in order to parent my brother in a way that was culturally acceptable at the time. She still remembers hiding in a closet to breastfeed him.

As he got older, my brother suffered from severe depression and substance abuse issues, which cost him his life when he was 25 years old.

Of course, my brother's fate could have been the same no matter how he was raised, but my parents carry the burden of questioning their choices and knowing that they didn't follow their instincts.

When I came along, my parents raised me completely by instinct, regardless of what was considered "appropriate" for the time. And when my sister had her children, even though she was not parented in this way, she followed attachment parenting because she saw me thriving.

Now I'm a parent, and it's my turn to make the decisions that will help shape my children. My education in anthropology afforded me fascinating insights into how natural selection shaped my children's behavior and my bond with my kids. I've also had some extraordinary opportunities as a parent, not the least of which is having been welcomed into the pioneering family of attachment parenting—Dr. William Sears, his wife Martha, and their incredible children.

My personal and professional experiences have led me to the firm belief that (1) attachment parenting is a wonderful way to raise children and (2) anybody can do it. My goal for this book is to show you how raising a well-attached child can be a joyful and totally manageable experience for all kinds of parents.

Granted, attachment parenting may seem more intimidating for those who do not fit into the mold of a typical nuclear family, because society has made it harder for you to get your bearings and find joy in parenting. I want you to know that I see you, I hear you, I support you, and I have been there. Whatever your story is, I want to help you thrive during the most human experience that you'll ever have: parenting.

SOMETIMES LIFE HAS OTHER PLANS

When I had Aram, my first child, I delivered him two months early via an emergency C-section having developed a rare but deadly condition in my pregnancy called HELLP syndrome. I couldn't visit him in the neonatal intensive care unit for three days because of my own health issues and recovery. At the time, I didn't know that you could recreate some of the key bonding that happens at birth. I felt like I had lost an important opportunity to connect with him, which was compounded by the post-traumatic stress disorder that resulted from a mismanaged emergency birth. During the following two years, I suffered from severe postpartum depression, which I'll talk more about as we delve into the importance of balance and boundaries in attachment parenting.

Despite my mental health challenges, amazing things happened in my life. In 2010, we welcomed home our second son, Samuel, adopted from Ethiopia at the age of four. Samuel is older than Aram by a year and a half, and at the time I believed creating the kind of attachments I wanted to foster in my children would be an uphill battle. How could you birth bond or babywear a four-year-old?

But we did. I bonded with premature Aram in the postpartum through steadfastly guarding my space during the "fourth trimester" period, babywearing, and cosleeping. I was able to breastfeed four-year-old Samuel in tandem with Aram, which helped to nurture his bond with me and, to my surprise, helped communicate to Aram that Samuel's role in his life was "brother" in a way words could not.

As we move through the various aspects of the attachment parenting lifestyle, I will share pieces of my unique journey with you. But, let's be clear: I'm not going to pretend I have it all figured out or that I'm a perfect parent whose life is amazing because I picked the Correct Way to Parent™. There is no one way to practice attachment parenting. No one practices all of the tools associated with AP 100 percent of the time. None of us have it all together. I have moments when I feel like an utter failure at motherhood and at life, even as I write this book.

What I am confident in though are lots of lessons learned. Things I wish I could go back and tell myself as a young mom. We all just do what we can, and attachment parenting is a philosophy that leans into that. I hope that at least some of it will help you and your family find a version of this parenting style that works for you. I invite you to take what you find helpful and leave the rest. Think of it as an a la carte buffet.

Of course, AP families aren't immune to divorce. In 2015, my marriage fell apart, and I became a single attachment parent/co-parent. I've never been more grateful for the strong attachment that I built with my children than the days when we are apart. There is a huge misconception that cosleeping and responsive parenting ruin your marriage. Ironically, our marriage was the strongest when our children were little and we were closely following the attachment parenting path. However, this new experience of being a single parent opened me up to many of the difficulties that single attachment parents face. Throughout the book I'll address these difficulties and provide some solutions that helped me.

I'll share my experience during the past 15 years working in various areas of the world, where parenting is viewed very differently than it is in the West. I'll take you through how to look at the unique needs of our children and our families and hopefully help you accept that we as a culture are imperfect. There are many ways to parent well, but there are no ways to parent perfectly. The best we can do is trust the instincts that nature has placed within us and find the ways of parenting that work for our unique situations.

Throughout this book I will be referring here and there to the "Village," with a capital "V." This is not any Village in particular, or even a real place. It's an acknowledgement that humans evolved under cooperative parenting conditions, not the isolated conditions that we see in the West, where help only comes if it's hired out. We can't bring the Village back, but we can build a new one. The Village is not so much a place as a promise we make to each other, to take care of each other.

MOM ENOUGH: PARENTING THROUGH JUDGEMENT

As parents, we're constantly judged for our choices, and as attachment parents, sometimes more so. In 2012 I agreed to be on the cover of *Time* magazine breastfeeding my youngest child, then age three, in an attempt to alleviate the many misconceptions around attachment parenting. I was not prepared for how explosive the issue would turn out to be.

It ended up being one of the best-selling issues of all time, and it painted me as a poster child for this sort of parenting. It also stirred up a lot of conversation surrounding this issue—the article's headline "Are You Mom Enough?" received a ton of backlash, and I was personally under intense scrutiny for extended breastfeeding. My young family was followed by TMZ demanding that I answer for the entire attachment parenting community.

For me, the biggest barrier to success in bonding with my children was my anxiety. I didn't get the help I needed, when I needed it, and it prevented me from bonding with them the way I feel like I could have. All of that anxiety was refocused in the weeks and months after my appearance on the cover of *Time* magazine. At the time, I was still experiencing the aftershocks of my traumatic birth with Aram. I can see now the ways it interfered with the continued development of my bond with my children, including pulling me away from wanting to breastfeed Aram, because I was so traumatized by people's criticism of that very thing.

Thankfully, I didn't stop breastfeeding Aram. Instead, I focused on the instincts and belief system that had driven me to embrace attachment parenting in the first place. The takeaway was so much more than "Don't let anyone tell you how long you can breastfeed." On a broader level, it gave me the confidence to say, "Don't let anyone tell you what's right for your family. You're the parent."

How to Use This Book

Attachment parenting (AP) is a set of science-based tools for raising a more compassionate, resilient child.

Psychological research has shown that an infant's wants and needs are one and the same and that consistently meeting those needs builds empathy, trust, and emotional security. The relationship built between the child and parent is called attachment, and by evaluating the quality of the *attachment,* scientists have been able to predict the quality of the grown child's interpersonal relationships years down the road. This scientific model is called *attachment theory.*

Based on this science, Dr. William Sears developed a set of tools to help parents meet their baby's core needs. He named them the "Baby B's." In *The Baby Book,* published in 1993, Dr. Sears listed five tools, and he added two more in the 2001 edition, bringing the grand total number of Baby B's to seven.

This book is meant to empower parents with information, not burden them with rules. If you start to feel burdened, go back to the last B: balance. Gaining a deeper understanding of your child and the context in which you're attempting to raise him is therapeutic in and of itself, even if in the end you do nothing different at all. This understanding will allow you to let go of some of the guilt or uncertainty surrounding your choice to embrace attachment parenting. Once you have a good handle on why you are choosing to parent this way, you will be able to act with conviction and authority, even in the face of judgement.

Throughout the book you may come across terminology that is new to you, so be sure to check the Glossary at the back for definitions and more information.

THE BABY B'S

Birth bonding: This includes advance planning for the birth experience you want, which will ensure immediate contact at birth and minimal interference (page 23).

Breastfeeding: Nursing at the breast is wonderful for many reasons, but recognizing that it not always possible, we'll explore how to optimize the bottle feeding experience (page 7).

Babywearing: Keeping your baby close in a sling or wrap offers the benefit of touch and allows you to respond quickly to his needs (page 8).

Bedding close to baby: Cosleeping has many options. You can have a cosleeper bed, which keeps baby in her own space next to you, or simply bring her crib into your bedroom (page 9).

Belief in the language value of your baby's cry: Your baby is communicating with you, not trying to manipulate you. It's your job to figure out what your baby is saying and to respond effectively (page 10).

Beware of baby trainers: Baby training is a behavioral intervention designed to modify babies' behavior to make it more convenient for Western life. This training can interfere with crucial brain development (page 11).

Balance: This is the most underreported and underappreciated of the Baby B's. The Searses know that AP can be very intense in a culture that is not friendly to non-authoritarian parenting styles. Dr. Sears then added this Baby B to the mix to highlight the importance of the family's well-being as a whole and the need for common sense (page 13).

In this book, I am grouping the Baby B's into four categories based on the main needs that they meet.

Bonding: Chapter 2 addresses the need for bonding, which is met by the first Baby B, birth bonding. I understand that some families adopt and some families miss out on birth bonding due to medical procedures, so I'll use the more inclusive term *early bonding.*

Nutrition and Nurturing: Chapter 3 addresses the baby's dual-need for nutrition and nurturing, which is met by the second Baby B, breastfeeding. However, as Western countries lag in supporting and enabling breastfeeding, a way forward for bottle feeding families is necessary. We'll discuss how breastfeeding is about more than the milk and how this knowledge can empower bottle feeding families in fostering a healthy attachment.

Contact: Chapter 4 discusses the two Baby B's that are oriented around physical space and meet baby's need for physical contact and proximity: babywearing and bedding close to baby (cosleeping). Both of these Baby B's can look very different for different families, and both can be amazing for helping rewrite your narrative and reclaim lost time and experiences, especially if you missed out on birth bonding or breastfeeding.

Communication: Chapter 5 addresses crying as a form of communication, which is what the Searses mean by the fifth Baby B: "Belief in the language value of baby's cries." We'll talk about how to decode this language and address the sixth Baby B: beware of baby trainers.

These middle chapters are supported by Chapter 1—which is a crash course in attachment parenting philosophy—and Chapter 6—which will address your remaining questions about making AP work while keeping your sanity intact.

THE OXYGEN MASK METAPHOR

As parents, we're constantly being told that self-care is important and that we must incorporate it to be healthy. Although the sentiment is well meaning, sometimes finding time for self-care feels impossible when we're deep in the trenches of parenting. Can you relate? If so, consider that caring for yourself is beneficial—and necessary—for your entire family.

You know the analogy about putting on your oxygen mask before you help others? Before every flight, the attendants instruct adults to put on their oxygen masks prior to assisting young children. This is for the safety of both parties: No one will be saved if the adult passes out halfway through assisting the child. The oxygen mask analogy applies to almost all aspects of parenting.

Parenting in Western society is often structured in a way that isolates the primary caregiver. Everyone's busy. Everyone's working. And it seems that nobody has time anymore. It's not uncommon for new parents to experience burnout, which can fuel mild depression (the baby blues) or more severe forms of postpartum depression (PPD), postpartum psychosis (PPP), or post-traumatic stress disorder (PTSD). I'll offer ways to protect your emotional well-being and share important early warning signs of postpartum mood disorders (see page 38).

A history of previous and existing mental health conditions puts you at greater risk of developing PPD and its related illnesses. If you have mental health concerns, you'll want to do a risk assessment with your doctor and develop a wellness plan before you become pregnant. Look for a health-care provider (or a team of providers) who will advocate for your overall well-being, rather than directing you toward one-size-fits-all maternal health care. A health-care professional can advise you on how to continue, add to, or wean from any psychotropic medications during pregnancy and/or breastfeeding. The right provider is crucial if you hope to breastfeed, as not all specialists are up to date on medication and breastfeeding, so some providers may advise women to stop taking a drug that is, in fact, compatible with breastfeeding. The National Institutes of Health keeps a database of breastfeeding drug compatibility called LactMed, which is listed in the Resources section of this book. You and your physician are the only ones qualified to make decisions based on the unique needs of your family and any specific health conditions you and/or your co-parent may have.

One of the common myths about attachment parenting is that it is all or nothing, but, in fact, very few parents consistently practice all the components of AP. For example, many of the Baby B's require close physical contact with babies and small children, and since some children have a more intense need for physical contact than others, many parents are left feeling touched out, or needing a physical break. This is normal, and we'll talk about it later in Chapter 6.

Other parents may have difficulty with cosleeping due to the restrictive size of their apartment. Some may not be able to babywear as much as they would like because they have a disability or live in a hot climate. They may have had breast surgery, or they may have physical restrictions related to their gender identity that make breastfeeding extremely difficult or impossible. Some parents may have sexual trauma, in which case I would encourage them to get support from a caring professional with expertise in this area. However, none of these issues reflect who you are as a parent, and all of these difficulties have workarounds that can make AP work for your unique family.

Although there may be physical obstacles to some components of attachment parenting, the majority of the barriers are social. AP works in harmony with our evolved biology. Our species requires an intense emotional and practical investment in the early years in order to optimize outcomes later in childhood and adulthood. In the context of Western culture, these investments can be a challenge. Think about this: Many attachment parents who have a desire to breastfeed beyond young babyhood are perceived as immodest or permissive. Attachment parents view young children's need for physical contact as normal and healthy, yet babies are unwelcome in many public spaces and workplaces. Attachment parents want permission to follow their instincts and sleep close to their children, but society tells them that it is sexually deviant or permissive or even that they will harm their baby by doing it.

In all these cases, parents are treated as if they aren't intelligent or qualified enough to make an informed decision. We will talk about these social barriers to the Baby B's with the intention of helping you release feelings of guilt and shame and move on with confidence and a solid game plan.

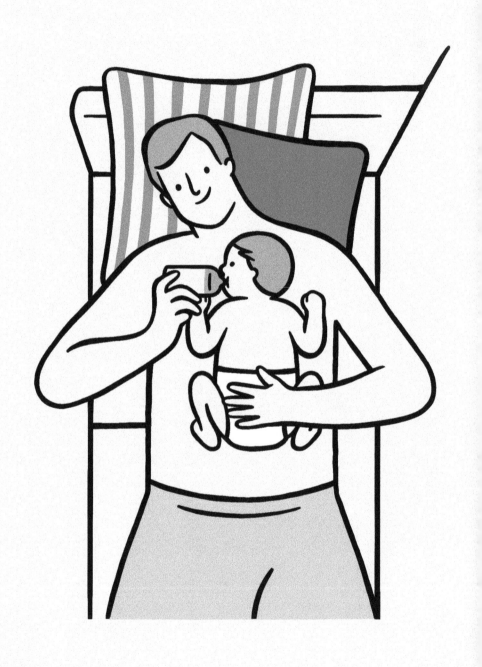

CHAPTER ONE

WHAT IS ATTACHMENT PARENTING?

Attachment parenting (AP) is a set of science-based tools for raising a more compassionate, emotionally secure child. Attachment parenting takes knowledge from attachment theory—an area of psychological research that focuses on emotional security and human relationships—and translates this knowledge into actionable items that parents can implement to help them raise an emotionally healthy child.

The Baby B's, which I will explore more in depth, are a set of tools that help the parent develop two main mental parenting skills:

> Sensitivity: the ability to accurately identify the needs of the child
> Responsivity: the ability to meet those needs consistently and with appropriate timing

As the parent learns to read her child accurately and respond effectively, the child learns to communicate his needs more effectively. Working together in a sort of dance, you create a secure base—that is, you become the child's safe space to which they may retreat for reassurance and comfort in times of stress and uncertainty. This safe-space relationship is called an *attachment.*

Attachment is different from bonding. A bond is a feeling of love or care for another person and is mostly about the person who is experiencing the feeling. Attachment is about the relationship between two people that is built over time through a lot of hard work and loving care.

Babies can have attachments to several people in their social circle, but the strongest predictors of outcomes are the attachments they have to their primary caregivers. Most American children have between one and four primary caregivers. If you are unsure who a child's primary caregivers are, here's a good rule of thumb: If the child is hurt or scared, whom do they run to first? That's their primary attachment figure.

Don't worry if you are a working parent or if you have a nanny or daycare provider—you still matter most to your child. The 2006 NICHD Study of Early Child Care and Youth Development indicated that in the vast majority of cases, even children who spend more time with their nannies than their own parents still run to their parent when they are hurt or scared. In the early months and years of life the brain is growing very rapidly, doubling in size over the first year. During this time, babies have very intense and constant physical needs and it tends to be the parent who does that work. This is one of the reasons nighttime parenting is so important, and why many working parents choose to cosleep. Stay confident in the attachment you've built and encourage attachment to the child's allo-parental caregivers; evidence suggests that secure attachments to multiple caregivers is healthy for development, and can actually help to reinforce the parental attachment.

Scientists have found that high-quality caregiver attachment leads to better outcomes for the child later on in life as it helps the child develop these skills:

Empathy: the ability to recognize and understand other people's feelings and to share in those feelings

- leads to higher quality relationships
- leads to positive social behavior
- leads to greater emotional security (i.e., "I am worth loving")

Resilience: persistence in the face of adversity

- fosters a strong work ethic and persistence in solving problems
- helps the child bounce back from setbacks (rejection, loss, failure) easier and faster

Emotional regulation: a way for humans to calm their nervous systems. Babies do this by co-regulating with their caretakers, which sets them up to self-regulate later.

- contributes to the quality of interpersonal relationships
- helps the child focus and fosters fruitful learning
- reduces chances of developing mental health challenges later in life

At its core, AP is about treating children the way you want them to treat others. A child's job is to learn how to exist in this world with other humans, and children learn most readily from the behaviors of those around them. By meeting our children's needs during crucial stages of brain development, we establish the security and behavioral prowess they need to develop positive relationships later in life.

What often catches parents off guard is how to navigate a world that is both overtly and covertly unfriendly to attachment parenting. The goals of attachment parenting are clear. The attachment parenting path, though trod by parents before us (whether they realized it or not), has grown over, and it is a little unclear in some places and quite treacherous in others. I'm here, machete in hand, to help clear the path for you. In case that sounds a little fierce, I'll explain.

AP parents are a tiny minority in the West, and as such, we are constantly bombarded with messages that are the exact opposite of what we want to be doing as parents. This counterintuitive messaging causes parents to question their choices and makes them wonder if they're babying their child too much, creating an overly dependent child, or being permissive.

One of the scientific strengths of attachment theory is that it was based on real-world, cross-cultural observations and then brought into the lab and put to the test. Beginning in the 1960s, British psychologist John Bowlby, along with other psychologists including Harry Harlow and Konrad Lorenz, noticed some patterns. Across cultures, children typically attach to their primary caregivers, experience intense distress when separated from the caregivers, and are wary of strangers. In the 1970s, one of Bowlby's students, Mary Ainsworth, developed a simple test by which attachment could be measured in the lab. Over the next few decades, children were followed as they grew, more longitudinal studies were conducted, and scientific support for attachment theory mounted.

You will notice that a lot of the Baby B's are oriented around physical contact—wearing your baby, sleeping physically close to your baby, and, of course, breastfeeding. Physical contact is important because, in the early months at least, a baby's emotional needs are one and the same with their physical needs.

It may seem counterintuitive, but the science tells us that this early dependence leads to greater independence later on. Scientists think that this is because, through reliably meeting the child's needs, you build your baby's brain for a world that is safe and will meet his needs if he puts in the effort.

COPING WITH DELAYED BONDING

The distinction between attachment and bonding becomes particularly important for parents who do not feel bonded to their babies right away, which is quite common in the West. Fathers most often struggle with not immediately feeling bonded to their babies, but mothers, especially those with postpartum mental health complications or recovering from a traumatic birth experience, deal with this as well. Please know that your feelings are not a reflection on you or your ability to love your baby. Regardless of whether you feel anything toward your child, the good news is that babies' attachment needs are straightforward in the newborn stage—your baby wants closeness and physical comfort. By meeting those basic needs, you will start to build an attachment with your baby. While you work through your own feelings toward your child, you can rest assured that your baby thinks the world of you.

THE BABY B'S

In the 1980s and 1990s, Dr. Sears and his wife Martha Sears, a nurse, worked together to adapt attachment theory for parents. The Searses wanted to help parents raise kinder, more resilient children who had fulfilling social and emotional lives. Meanwhile, attachment theory researchers John Bowlby and Mary Ainsworth were noticing two parental behaviors that were particularly strong predictors of attachment quality: *sensitivity* and *responsivity*.

Sensitivity refers to the ability to accurately recognize a child's needs, and responsivity refers to the parent's ability to consistently meet those needs. Researchers noticed that there are several parenting practices that inherently meet many of children's strongest needs. In his book *Touching: The Human Significance of the Skin,* Ashley Montagu lays out the mammalian universal that children's number one need is touch, and their second need is closeness/proximity. Researchers also noticed practices that tend to improve parents' sensitivity and responsivity by teaching parents to pay close attention to their child.

Most APers, particularly those in Western culture, cannot practice all the Baby B's 100 percent of the time. But keep the big picture in mind: When it comes to attachment parenting, your touch is their primary need, so every family has the ability to build a high-quality attachment with their child and have a fulfilling parenthood experience, no matter their circumstances.

Of course, many variables—including genetics—factor into outcomes. The science does not say, "If you do X, you will get result Y." Instead, think of attachment parenting in terms of increasing your child's odds at having a better life. There are no guarantees that practicing all the Baby B's religiously will result in a perfect child, any more than missing out on them will doom your child to a life of misery.

BIRTH/EARLY BONDING

Birth is a crucial period for both mother and baby, which is why the Searses strongly encourage parents to develop a birth plan. Mammalian birth is a long-evolved system, shaped by natural selection over the course of 35 million years, and, for us, even more finely tuned over the past few million years. An orchestra of neurotransmitters works in concert to establish the parent-infant bond, thus shaping maternal behavior toward the newborn and ultimately maximizing chances of survival for the infant.

In US hospitals, however, childbirth is treated like a disease or injury rather than a normal physiological process. Although medical intervention in birth has, to a degree, improved safety, many scientists are becoming concerned that excessive use of sensory stressors, such as noise, the presence of strangers poking and prodding with needles, and physical separation of the baby from the parents after birth, are interrupting these long-evolved systems and compromising parent-infant health, particularly as it applies to breastfeeding.

Many birth experts compare childbirth to two other sensitive functions: defecation and sex. If you had a doctor in the room, hooking you up to IVs, giving you drugs, shining bright lights in your eyes while you were carrying out these bodily functions, how do you think you would be affected?

Traditional attachment parenting resources emphasize that, with advance research and planning, parents can minimize their exposure to unnecessary procedures and maximize the use of the crucial golden hour after birth, when the neonate is chemically primed for bonding and feeding. This is what Dr. Sears refers to as the first Baby B: birth bonding.

Like many other parents, I was not present for the first hour of either of my children's lives. It's important to acknowledge that if you've already had your baby or if your choices in childbirth are limited for any reason, you can still recreate many of those golden hour benefits. This is exactly why we will be using the more inclusive term *early bonding.* Although birth itself is undeniably a unique biological process, you can think of early bonding as mostly serving to help set up the family for success in the coming weeks and months. We will talk about how techniques like kangaroo care, responsive feeding, and different forms of cosleeping can allow you to capture any bonding experiences that you're concerned you missed out on and help boost your confidence as a parent.

BREASTFEEDING

Breastfeeding is about so much more than just food. It is a system of adaptations that forms the core of mammalian physiology and the foundation for social development—a quintessentially natural and diversely beneficial experience. Yes, breastfeeding consists of biological components like nutrition, immune support, and a continuation of some aspects of fetal development through recently discovered stem cells found in human milk. But it also consists of a set of back-and-forth behaviors—known as reciprocity—between the parent and the child that foster the development of emotional regulation and early communication, which lay the foundation for effective discipline later on. As parents of older nurslings will tell you, this effect is thrown into sharp relief every time they stop a meltdown in its tracks with a quick nurse! These behavioral components may explain many of the the social benefits of breastfeeding. We'll focus on these components when we talk about how to feed formula or donated milk in a bottle to your baby.

BABYWEARING

Babywearing is probably the least controversial component of attachment parenting and the easiest one to implement. Babywearing is also the most popular—many parents do not even realize they're practicing attachment parenting. This component meets the infant or young child's strong need for physical contact and allows a nursling easier access to the breast.

Since being held is comforting, wearing your baby puts her in a calm alert state—the perfect state for learning. Babies who are worn by their caregivers have been shown to cry less than babies who are not. But perhaps the most popular reason people wear their babies is because it frees up the caregivers' hands, allowing them to meet baby's needs while getting other things done.

We'll talk about how to choose a carrier, how to bottlenurse a baby in a baby carrier, what to do if you live in a hot climate, how to find a carrier appropriate for your size, what to do if you have a physical restriction, how to deal with a baby who is carrier resistant, and other ways you can meet your baby's need for physical contact when you are not able to wear your child.

BEDDING CLOSE TO BABY

Throughout human evolution, sleep has been an intensely social activity for humans. For most of human history, houses only had one room, and in many cultures, families still share a bed. However, as people in the West became more affluent, separate rooms for sleep and other activities spread beyond the royal elite and became standard for us regular folks.

In the mid-20th century, safety recommendations began to shift towards separate sleep for infants. However, babies, as you might have guessed, never got the memo. Babies continue to have a strong need for physical touch and proximity in the nighttime, just as they do in the daytime. Cosleeping is an invitation to work with that evolved biology.

What many people don't realize is that cosleeping comes in many forms. Babies and older children around the world sleep with their mothers, fathers, aunts, uncles, grandmothers, grandfathers, and older siblings. They do so in hammocks, in hanging cradles, on Japanese futons, on mats on the floor, on the same surface as someone else, or across the room.

In the West, some cosleeping families have a family bed. We will explore the options and discuss infant safety as it pertains to bed sharing and cosleeping (see page 75). Other families may have a cosleeper or a bassinet in the parents' room, put an adult bed or mattress in the child's room and switch off between parents, or put the baby to bed in the nursery, then bring him back to bed with them halfway through the night. There are many versions of cosleeping, and one of them is sure to work for your family. There are also ways to meet your baby's nighttime needs if she sleeps alone. Later, we'll talk about how babies' need for closeness at night is normal and healthy, as is their resistance to solitary sleep.

BELIEF IN THE LANGUAGE VALUE OF BABY'S CRIES

Our babies are born uniquely helpless compared to other mammals. They can't text you from their crib to let you know that they are too warm, their diaper is dirty, or they need to be reassured that you haven't abandoned them. Belief in your baby's cry is the idea that a baby's needs and wants are the same and that no baby cries to manipulate you.

When an infant cries, her nervous system is signaling genuine distress. Even if her life is not threatened, her limbic system (reptilian brain) doesn't know that. Stress hormone levels will increase in her blood regardless of the issue. Responding to babies' cries quickly and accurately helps keep their stress levels low and primes their brains to react in healthy ways to the normal stresses of the world. A baby who is left to cry often will have a brain that develops for a stressful world, and he may grow up to be overly reactive to stressors and struggle to recover from emotional challenges such as death, loss, or major events, like moving or changing jobs.

This Baby B is one in which sensitivity and responsivity really come into play. Parents experience a detectable neurological reaction to the sound of their infant's cry. Well-attached parents can listen to their baby's cry, watch his body language, and tell you with greater accuracy what the baby needs. These parents will also be more strongly motivated to respond to that need quickly every time, and they'll have a harder time tolerating prolonged crying. As you can imagine, responding consistently ends up being a lot of work. But this intense investment in the early years can pay off later, when you have a confident, emotionally resilient adult child.

Some families may have to deal with more crying than others. We will talk about what you can do to cope and mitigate the stressful effects of crying and what to do if you have a baby who cries in his car seat. We'll also discuss things like crying in restaurants, cars, and situations where you are unable immediately respond to crying.

BEWARE OF BABY TRAINERS

Babies are not born with a diurnal sleep schedule like we adults have (primarily awake during the day, asleep at night). Sleep is a developmental process that unfolds slowly over the first months and years of life. Adults wake up at night as well, but then they go back to sleep and may not remember waking up. Babies and small children, however, wake with greater frequency and need help falling back asleep. This is normal for humans in every culture. An infant's sleep structure is totally different than that of an adult, with more time spent in a lighter stage called *active sleep,* which is like rapid eye movement sleep. Particularly typical for breastfed babies, this lighter sleep, coupled with more frequent wakings, is part of what is believed to protect against sudden unexplained infant death, and sudden infant death syndrome, commonly known as SIDS.

In recent decades, however, research on adult sleep has been extrapolated, incorrectly, to infants and children. An entire industry of products and services designed to make babies sleep longer, harder, and deeper has emerged.

From an attachment parenting perspective, the issue with cry-it-out sleep training is that it is a behavioral intervention intended to treat a sleep disorder that babies, by and large, don't actually have. And in almost all cases, a disorder has not been diagnosed. As a culture, we are pathologizing perfectly normal human infant behavior. We don't yet fully know the long-term consequences of this approach, but, at minimum, the process is very stressful for the baby.

Attachment parenting is largely oriented toward responsivity, as discussed by Dr. Diane Benoit in a 2004 article for *Paediatrics*

& *Child Health,* which science has shown is associated with healthy emotional development. However, the defining feature of infant sleep training—not responding to an infant's cry—is the exact opposite of responsivity. But perhaps more than that, it is emotionally distressing to listen to a baby cry, and many families instinctively prefer not to hear their child cry.

So how does a desperate parent navigate nighttime parenting without sleep training? What if you already chose to sleep train and wonder how it may impact attachment and development? What if you work 80 hours a week and you feel like your life will fall apart if you take the time to rock your baby to sleep every night? We'll explore all of this and show you that in most cases, you have what it takes to get baby on a schedule. In Chapter 4, we will talk about evidence-based methods to improve both your and your baby's sleep quality (not just quantity). We'll discuss the role of anxiety in sleep and ways to help you feel more connected when you are awake.

We will also talk about a new, evidence-based sleep coaching program that is currently being field-tested and could be a game changer for parents who prefer not to let their babies cry. Perhaps most importantly, we will talk about the causes of parental burn-out—those rare moments when the safest option really is to put the baby down and walk away—the guilt and shame surrounding sleep, how we all make mistakes, and how we can move on from them with confidence.

BALANCE/BOUNDARIES

This is the Baby B that media critics of attachment parenting always seem to ignore. In reading the media discourse on AP, you'd never even know that Dr. Sears ever wrote about balance. Every single one of the major Sears books says, "IF YOU RESENT IT, CHANGE IT." (Yes, the Searses write it in all capitals.) The authors point out that practicing this intense style of parenting will stretch you, but it shouldn't snap you. They realistically acknowledge that not every Baby B can be practiced by every family all the time. The Searses encourage taking breaks, asking for help, and reminding yourself that "what your baby needs most is a happy, rested [parent]."

In this book, I offer my perspective as a millennial parent on practicing AP in a modern cultural milieu that often doesn't accommodate this "paleo" style of parenting. You will not necessarily be able to do all the Baby B's all the time, and I hope I've made it clear that that's okay. Understand that many of your struggles will not be a result of your choice to attachment parent but a result of a culture that is actively hostile to this choice. I can't say I will totally rid you of your internal struggles or your parent guilt, but hopefully a deeper understanding of the benefits of all you are already doing will give you peace of mind and enable you to be a little kinder to yourself.

COMMON MYTHS AND MISCONCEPTIONS ABOUT AP

In the wake of my appearance on the cover of *Time* magazine, I went through a crash course in the media discourse surrounding attachment parenting and the science behind it. Many stereotypes, myths, and misconceptions have muddied the waters of truth, and so I'd like to dispel some of them here.

MYTH: "Attachment parenting is unscientific."

REALITY: Attachment parenting is based on attachment theory—a highly tested scientific paradigm for explaining many social and behavioral phenomena. Attachment theory is widely recognized in psychological science as a strong predictor of several social outcomes. Critics will note that there are no studies that have investigated attachment parenting as a philosophy and whether it works. This is because APers vary in their ability to carry out all of the Baby B's, from family to family and from moment to moment, making this sort of broad study impractical. The individual Baby B's, however, have been studied, and have each been found to contribute to increased parental sensitivity and responsivity, which we know influences attachment quality. The Baby B's, then, do influence outcomes in an indirect manner.

MYTH: "Attachment parenting is permissive parenting."

REALITY: This myth comes out of the idea that it is possible to "spoil" a baby and that constantly carrying a baby or nursing beyond infancy is spoiling the child. These ideas are perpetuated by the way breast-feeding is sometimes portrayed in the media. Babies and small children have a strong emotional drive to sleep with their parents, breastfeed, and be held, and they often cry when they can't have those things. It's natural, as is our urge to respond. Due to AP's highly responsive nature, it is probably true that permissive-leaning parents may take to AP more readily than authoritarian-leaning parents. However, while a permissive-leaning parent may take readily to responsivity, they might not be a particularly sensitive parent, and accurately identifying a child's true need (distinct from their wants) is a core skill in attachment parenting.

MYTH: "Only mothers can be attached to their child."

REALITY: The Searses' opinion on the mother-child relationship has evolved over the years in response to newer cross-cultural research that shows that many hunter-gatherer societies pass their babies around from person to person, sometimes shortly after the child's birth. Edward O. Wilson coined the term *alloparenting* to refer to the other adults in an infant animal or human child's life who help care for them. Primatologist and Darwinian feminist Sarah Blaffer Hrdy is a wonderful writer who tied this community approach to childrearing to evolution and the behavior of our primate cousins.

It is important to note, though, that in these cultures where babies are cared for by multiple community members, the culture around children is also very different. In these tight-knit communities, the child can expect alloparents to be in their lives for the long-term. Babies are often cross-nursed, the entire culture accepts the intense physical needs of children and small babies as normal—responding quickly is the norm. Historically and cross-culturally, allocare is not performed by paid institutions but by members of the community who are well known to the child and care for the child in a highly responsive manner.

MYTH: "Attachment parenting is anti-feminist."

REALITY: If so many of the needs of infants are physical—and in the case of breastfeeding and birthing, place physical burdens on the mother's body—it makes complete sense that attachment parenting may seem oppressive to some. And indeed, deployed wrongly and in the wrong context, this area of science can and is used to control women's bodies—such as in the context of religious extremism, where women's bodies are regarded as baby-making factories. Evolutionary feminist and primatologist Sarah Blaffer Hrdy writes a good deal on this topic in her book *The Woman That Never Evolved*. I am fighting for a world in which the choice to breastfeed or cosleep in a safe way is fully accepted and supported by an informed society and made as easy as possible. We forget that the resurgence of breastfeeding and home birth was spearheaded by the feminist movements of the 1960s and 1970s. Many women, in fact, feel that breastfeeding is a radical feminist act—it is reclaiming their bodies from a patriarchal society that views their bodies as purely sexual objects that exist only for the pleasure of men and the selling of products. Kimberly Seals Allers notes that for many African American women, breastfeeding is a way to rewrite their narratives and to take back the larger narrative from a history where their enslaved ancestors were made to wet-nurse the babies of their captors while their own babies were ripped from their arms.

MYTH: "Attachment parenting makes your children too emotionally dependent on you and doesn't prepare them for the world."

REALITY: It seems counterintuitive, but this "indulgent" form of parenting actually helps children achieve independence. There is a strong emphasis in American parenting culture on pushing independence earlier and earlier, but due to the deeply ingrained evolved neurology of the human infant, this push can backfire.

The best metaphor for how attachment works in children is that consistently meeting the child's needs early on creates a secure base from which they can venture out into the world and explore. The child wades a little out into the water, then retreats to the parent for reassurance and comfort. Sometimes, the child may just glance back in the parent's direction. As time goes on, the child ventures farther and farther, retreating to the parent less and less often. The process will vary because child temperaments vary. If you translate this analogy into all of child rearing and serve as a present and responsive support to your child, by the time the child is older, she will be more self-assured and emotionally resilient than she otherwise would have been. In the teenage years, these children will generally be able to take on greater responsibilities, be less susceptible to peer pressure, and recover better from their first breakup or snub by a friend than children who have not been raised according to this style.

MYTH: "Attachment parenting is all or nothing."

REALITY: I don't think I've ever met a parent who practices all the Baby B's all the time. Most of the research on the Baby B's—breastfeeding, in particular—has found what scientists call a dose-response effect, which means that the more you practice a behavior, the greater effect it is likely to have. This effect also means that every little bit counts. If you can cosleep part-time, great. If you managed to get your hospital to delay some of the after-birth interventions but not all of them, great. If you've managed to make mixed feeding work, great. Your child will benefit from all of it.

It's important to remember that attachment parenting is made more difficult by a culture that does not necessarily understand, accept, and support this parenting style. I want to help you work within whatever parameters your life allows. If you believe in raising a child who is compassionate, resilient, and emotionally secure and you do your best to achieve that goal, then I hereby declare that you are allowed to call yourself an attachment parent.

MYTH: "Attachment parenting is only for 'crunchy' parents."

REALITY: If you think you have an idea in your head about what an attachment parent looks like, you can scribble over it with a big black crayon. The people who practice AP run the gamut just like everyone else. Some vaccinate, and some don't. They're high-powered attorneys and physicists. APers include parents who eat organic and those who don't care as long as it's fresh. They live in Colorado and in Los Angeles. Some are strict disciplinarians, and some are more lenient. APers use bleached tampons and biodegradable diapers. These parents are Christian and atheists, and some don't think about religion much at all. Some don't let their kids see a single screen before age two, and others put their kids in front of screens all the time. APers take their kids to chiropractors and give their kids antibiotics.

They put breast milk on everything from pink eye to knee scrapes. Some of them had a home birth, and some of them had an elective C-section. Almost all of them love a little fast food sometimes. You get the gist.

There's nothing in the attachment parenting books about GMOs or essential oils—and no granola.

MYTH: "Attachment parents are helicopter parents."

REALITY: AP is an intense physical investment (but so is any parenting) that requires sensitivity to the child's emotional needs. However, attachment parenting is distinctly countercultural, so AP parents are also more likely to be attracted to some of the hands-off parenting movements that have emerged as a reaction to helicopter parenting. You may have heard of free-range parenting, idle parenting, and Respectful Infant Education, or RIE. All these philosophies emphasize a return to the 1960s, 1970s, and 1980s, when ideally, children roamed the neighborhood between the school bell and dinner, walked to school by themselves, and played outside often—without an adult supervising every move.

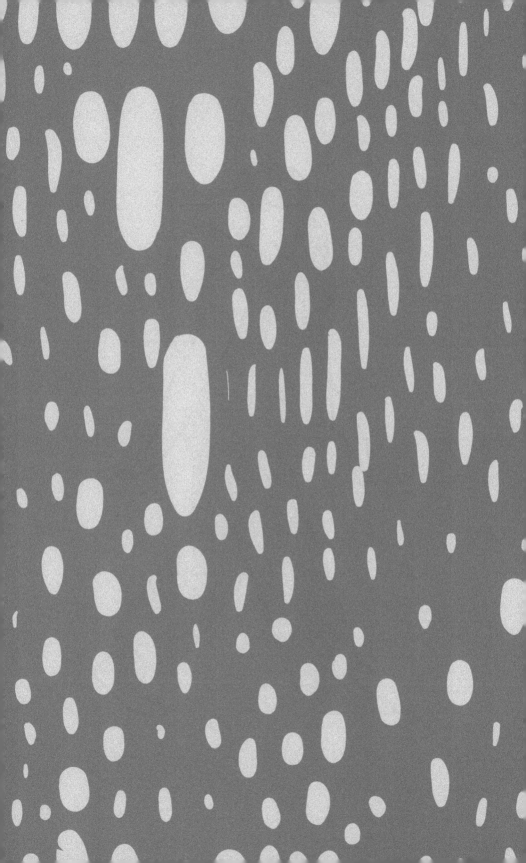

CHAPTER TWO

BOND, BABY, BOND

Childbirth is a uniquely human experience that relies on primal processes that were shaped by evolution under intense selective pressure. These processes work in both the baby and the birthing parent, but sometimes the processes can be interrupted or masked by Western birthing practices, particularly in the hospital setting.

In an uninterrupted context, babies and their birthing mother both undergo a dramatic flood of hormones in the minutes and hours immediately following the birth. After giving birth, the mother's body is flooded with endorphins that help ease the pain of childbirth, and oxytocin, which helps with bonding. The baby is flooded with adrenaline, which keeps him alert and active for the first hour after birth, and primed for learning how to feed, his first survival skill. As discussed, this first hour after birth is often referred to as the *golden hour.* Supporting skin-to-skin contact and breastfeeding during this period has been shown to support the establishment of breastfeeding and improve chances of success in the long term.

A little-known fact about this period is that a baby born to a mother who is given minimal analgesics during birth will do a sort of army crawl to the breasts. Amanda Henderson, a registered nurse and lactation consultant, described this phenomenon in a 2011 article for *Nursing for Womens Health Journal.* If a newborn is placed on the mother's abdomen immediately following birth, he'll even latch entirely on his own. Newborns are strongly attuned to their mother's pheromones. They're attracted to the high-contrast sight of the nipples and the smell of her milk, and over the course of the next 10 to 60 minutes, they'll wiggle around to get closer to the breasts. Feeling around with their arms and hands, they eventually reach a nipple with a hand, which triggers their grasping reflex. The baby then self-latches, with little or no help, and begins the first feed. This is known as the *breast crawl.*

Watching this process is an empowering experience for the mother because it is her first chance to see what her child is already capable of. The process also naturally instills a sense of confidence in her own ability, even as a brand-new parent, to provide for her baby and work together as a team. Psychologists Ariana Albanese, Gabrielle Russo, and Pamela Gellar describe this sense of confidence as *parental self-efficacy,* a known predictor of positive outcomes. Parental self-efficacy is more than just the feeling of, "Yes, I can parent this child." It's also a sense of, "Yes, I am worthy of parenting this child."

Positive, family-centered birth experiences are not just a nice idea. They can help set families up for success, particularly in breastfeeding, by taking advantage of intuitive biological processes like the breast crawl. In fact, most people don't end up executing their ideal birth plan. And while an uninterrupted birth process can make the establishment of breastfeeding and early bonding easier, not having the opportunity to do so does not make either one less possible.

BIRTH BONDING (EVEN IF YOU DIDN'T GIVE BIRTH)

Unfortunately, many hospital practices—some necessary, some arguably not so much—do not allow for uninterrupted physical contact and bonding after birth. Babies are often separated from their parents immediately following birth for routine procedures or medical emergencies. Almost all hospital-born babies are immediately given an antibacterial medication in their eyes that blurs their vision, and it's unknown how this medication impacts the baby's ability to see her parents' faces or locate the nipple for nursing. Breastfeeding difficulties, health complications, and lack of support can make families feel shortchanged out of some or all of the birth experiences they dreamed of. Many parents and families experience serious medical complications and miss out on not just the golden hour, but the entire birth bonding experience. That's okay. Mine was one of those families. We were able to reclaim our attachment once we came home from the hospital.

Sometimes, in the weeks and months after birth, families learn that some of the post-birth procedures, while important, were maybe not so urgent and could have waited until after the golden hour, which can make parents feel that they were unnecessarily separated from their baby after birth. If you haven't given birth yet, know that you have the right to be the first person to hold your own baby. With a lot of conflicting information, it can be a challenge to figure out which procedures are urgent and which ones can wait. For information about the scientific evidence for common post-birth interventions, I recommend Evidence Based Birth's website (see Resources, page 118).

SEPARATED AT BIRTH—MY STORY

I encourage efforts to actively support the bonding process, but at the same time, I don't want you to think you should feel any particular way immediately. My own experience with being separated from my baby is hardly a story of a fertility goddess aglow in post-birth ecstasy.

I couldn't see my son Aram for three days. Having been born prematurely, Aram was sent to the neonatal intensive care unit (NICU) after his birth while I was admitted to the ICU, heavily sedated, to allow my body to recover from HELLP syndrome. It was a very scary situation—my son and I were each hooked up to life-saving equipment in separate wards and could not be physically near each other.

Family support was crucial for me. My sister-in-law at the time, who is a pediatrician, went to the NICU to take a photo of my baby and brought it back to me because the visual stimuli of seeing your baby helps some women release their milk better. My now ex-husband did almost everything else. He took care of me and cleaned my pumping equipment and everything so that literally all I had to do was just sit there and pump milk. I was barely even conscious.

I am not sure how much that photo helped with my milk release. What was most helpful was it felt like a team effort directed toward making sure that this baby had milk, which everyone knew was very important to me. Also helpful, I think, was that everybody tried to make the situation as lighthearted and fun as possible, which made a very serious situation less scary for me. My sister-in-law kept reminding me that everything was going to be okay. And hey, let's try these tips and tricks for milk production! This picture thing is supposed to work, let's try it out. And if it works, great, but if it doesn't, everything is still going be okay. I felt really supported, like everyone had my back.

When the time finally came, meeting Aram wasn't really an amazing experience. He was perfect. Everyone in the NICU was telling me that he was doing great. But I was filled with feelings of guilt and shame because I felt like my body failed him. I gave birth to him so early, and it hadn't felt like a real pregnancy. It just felt like this massive failure. I felt like I couldn't finish the job, a job that my body was supposedly built for. And I felt that my baby suffered because of it. I didn't know then that bonding could look different for every family. I didn't know then that there are variables that can keep our brains and bodies from doing the instinctive work anthropology taught me. I didn't know then that I would come to have such an attached relationship with Aram and that our long-term bond wouldn't suffer because of our rough start.

KANGAROO CARE

The first and most helpful thing to do once you finally get your baby in your arms is *kangaroo care,* also known as *skin-to-skin.* Some people think of kangaroo care as just for preemies, but parents of term babies are increasingly requesting accommodations for post-birth kangaroo care due to the mountain of research that indicates this care supports breastfeeding and bonding. Kangaroo care is particularly helpful for newborns, regardless of the feeding method the parent plans to use, because it helps babies regulate their temperature. This way, every extra calorie can go to brain growth instead of temperature regulation. Kangaroo care is something that many parents discover on their own, often because dads are more likely to walk around the house with their shirt off. Quite by accident, dad will find that his bare chest is calming to the baby and very often where the baby sleeps best.

If the mother is getting a C-section, then have the dad/partner prepped and ready with a button-down shirt so they can take the baby for skin-to-skin contact. Adoptive parents can follow the same procedure if you are meeting your baby the hospital. Try to set up your adoption transfer so that you'll have a private room with a comfortable chair or bed where you can enjoy some kangaroo care together for at least an hour. If you are doing adoptive breastfeeding, get to work with a lactation consultant (look for the IBCLC certification after the name) as soon as you make the decision to breastfeed and arrange for the consultant to visit you at the hospital.

The procedure for kangaroo care is simple: Take off your shirt, or wear a button-down shirt that opens in front. Strip your baby down to her diaper and hold the baby, facing you, on your chest. A light blanket can be draped over baby's back, and a hat placed

on baby's head if it's chilly. Your body will help the baby regulate her temperature more efficiently than an incubator.

Before you sit down, it helps to set up a chair and arrange pillows in a way that allows you to comfortably recline at about a 45-degree angle. Rest there for as long as you like but note that you may find your-

self getting sleepy. If you think you may doze off while holding the baby, switch to a safe sleep environment on a firm mattress. Chairs, sofas, and pillows are not part of a safe cosleeping environment. We will talk about safe cosleeping practices later (see Resources, page 117).

Many parents find that kangaroo care is one of the things they enjoy most about early parenthood. Why not? Kangaroo care is relaxing, mindful, and lets parents feel a sense of connection with their baby. But kangaroo care is more than just quality cuddle time—it also helps babies regulate their body temperature, heart rate, and breathing. This regulation helps build their nervous system in a way that helps them better cope with stress later in life and stimulates oxytocin in their brain, which helps with digestion and growth. New parents experience an increase in oxytocin as well, which promotes feelings of closeness and relaxation and modifies the levels of other hormones, such as prolactin, which helps increase the parent's sensitivity toward the child and strengthens attachment.

Kangaroo care also facilitates breastfeeding in the newborn period. Many folks don't realize that babies retain their ability to do the breast crawl (page 22) throughout the newborn period. Newborns continue to be highly attuned to the smell of mother's milk, so being placed on the mom's bare chest is an intensely stimulating sensory experience for a newborn.

After birth, it's best to try kangaroo care at least an hour after the baby has been fed, when he's awake and alert but not yet crying. Find a comfy couch or bed and arrange some pillows that allow you to comfortably lie back at about a 45-degree angle. When baby is placed on your chest, you'll notice his movements become more coordinated, as opposed to the flailing movements a baby often does while lying on his back. And if you are very, very patient, the baby will self-attach to a nipple all on his own. Watching your baby achieve this feat will allow you to relive the pride and wonderment of those early bonding experiences. Called *dry nursing* for those (regardless of gender) who aren't lactating, this experience is a wonderful way to bond. Follow the process described above and let the contrast between your nipple and your skin guide the baby toward latch. For more about this laid-back breastfeeding approach, check out Nancy Mohrbacher's YouTube videos (see Resources, page 117).

In addition to plenty of kangaroo care, rooming-in and participating actively in the daily care of your baby while still in the hospital can help you get off to a good start. Particularly for partners, connecting with baby happens through spending time physically caring for her.

BEING COMFORTABLE IN YOUR SKIN

Here's a heads up: There are lots of weird little things that people don't anticipate while planning their postpartum recovery. One of those things is that a lot of moms find themselves almost completely nude for much of the time during the first couple of weeks after they've given birth. It is going to sound strange now, but in the first days and weeks after I came home with Aram, I found myself not wanting to wear clothes. I was leaking fluids and constantly needed to change my clothes anyway, so I kind of asked myself, "Why bother?"

If you don't feel like wearing clothes, just don't put them on. It isn't rude to lock yourself away in your bedroom if you feel like it. It's totally okay to spend as much time as you want naked and lying in your bed with your baby—for weeks after birth, if that's what you feel like doing. Do not feel obligated to cater to the needs of visitors—or even to entertain any at all.

Some parents feel differently and may be a little aversive to the idea of doing a good deal of kangaroo care because, by its very nature, it involves some degree of skin exposure. Often, parents will do kangaroo care in the hospital, but then go on with their normal, fully-clothed lives when they get home—especially when the guests start to arrive.

If you get home and start to feel reluctant to do kangaroo care, it might help to ask yourself, "Why, exactly, do I feel this way? Is it a religious belief? Am I shy about my body?" I encourage you to work through these feelings (preferably before giving birth, if you can), but you might also choose to limit visitors in the early weeks so that you can prioritize kangaroo care.

I encourage you to be proud of your body and what it can do. If you ask me, your body is amazing! It literally just built an entire person. Even if you didn't give birth, your body is providing the warmth and comfort that your baby needs to thrive. Tell guests that if they want to visit the baby, then get used to seeing some skin. And never, ever apologize for this.

IF YOU'RE A SINGLE PARENT AT BIRTH

For a single parent, birth can be a uniquely stressful time if you don't have a support system in place. Single parents in particular can benefit immensely from hiring a doula, if it's in the budget. There are doulas who specialize in birth as well as those who specialize in mothering the mother in the days and weeks following the birth. A postpartum doula can do what a partner would do or what your mother might not do in the way that you need her to. The doula's job is to provide practical and emotional support while you establish breastfeeding and bond with your baby. This support can range from throwing in a load of laundry to sitting with you and reassuring you that what you're feeling is normal to finding a strategically polite way of clueing in your overbearing aunt that it's time to leave. Having a doula is like having a visit from an older sister who's given birth 10 times and is here to see you, not the baby. A doula can also be a wonderful investment if you have physical or mental disabilities or other limitations that require you to have additional support. Interview doulas beforehand so you can find somebody who understands your needs, is easy to talk to, and offers supportive guidance. You can even seek out a doula who specializes in caring for new parents who are differently abled (see Resources, page 117).

If you are unsure about whether a postpartum doula is in the budget, note that many doulas offer a sliding scale. Alternatively, since attachment parenting tends to reduce the need for baby items like strollers and cribs anyway, consider asking for contributions to a doula fund in lieu of baby shower gifts.

ROOMING-IN

Rooming-in is the now common practice of keeping your baby's bassinet in your hospital room instead of sending your child to the nursery for the night. In addition to providing easier access for breastfeeding, research suggests that taking care of your own baby in the hospital lessens the shock of transitioning to the home. Also, having the chance to practice taking care of your baby with specialists at arm's reach gives you the opportunity to address any sticking points that you otherwise wouldn't run into until you were home.

Sometimes, though, medical complications prevent rooming-in. In that case, going about the everyday care of your baby during the daytime can give you a sense of agency over a situation that might otherwise feel a little disappointing or out of control.

You might ask, for example, if you can give the baby her first bath. Babies are often whisked off to the nursery for a bath, but there's no need to bathe your baby immediately after birth—the vernix covering the baby's skin contains a pheromone from the womb that you want to avoid interfering with if you plan to breastfeed.

When you do decide it's time to bathe your baby, it is a magical moment you won't want to miss out on, and not a task that requires any professional skills. Ask to have a warmer brought to your room, since babies often cry during a bath because they are cold. Alternatively, you can wrap the baby in a towel or blanket and unwrap one body part at a time and give your baby a sponge bath, one precious little roll at a time. Know that there is no urgency to the bath, and no medical reason it must be done on the day of the birth, other than personal preference. If you would rather have that time to spend together as a family, take it. It's yours.

If you are completely bedridden and separated from your baby for medical reasons, consider asking a family member or member of the hospital staff to take photo or video of your baby for you. A couple of minutes of video footage of baby in an awake state, either looking around or crying, might help set off the chemical reaction in your brain to facilitate bonding. If you are pumping, the sound of crying helps because the sounds that babies make—especially crying—help trigger the release of your milk. Experiment, if you can, to see what works for you. If something doesn't work for you, don't sweat it. Just move on to something else or take a break and try again another time.

WELCOME HOME!

Think of the first weeks and months at home with your baby as a baby-moon period. The general advice for the first month after giving birth is ideally 10 days in the bed, 10 days on the bed, and 10 days around the bed. This is your chance to spend all day doing kangaroo care and nursing that sweet little baby's brains out. It helps for some people to think of the weeks and months following birth as a fourth trimester, where mother's body is still experiencing major changes, and the baby is still attached to a sort of invisible umbilical cord.

There are many cultures around the world that have different traditions centered around the concept of a lying-in period. It sounds oppressive to say that the mom is hidden away in her bedroom, but it's not like that at all. It's more like a nesting period. Other mammals do this around the time of birth—you may remember the cat from your childhood who hid in a closet to give birth to her kittens. This is because mammals are drawn to dark, enclosed, safe spaces for birth and recovery. Now, this may come as a shock to you, but we are mammals, too. And many women behave in a remarkably similar way—retreating, relaxing, and recovering.

Generally, the lying-in period goes something like this: For a month or so after birth, the mother stays in her home, her bedroom, or a special woman-run location that serves this sacred purpose. She doesn't have any responsibilities at all, and it is the job of the community to treat her like a queen—they take care of her so that she can take care of the baby, recover from birth, and come in to her new identity as a mother.

Not everyone loves this idea, but I found that this was exactly what I wanted. I found that I did not want many visitors. I wanted a nice, clean space with low lights and very few visitors. I just wanted someone else to be there to bring me food and water and other basic necessities so I could lie around holding my baby.

Don't be afraid to ask extended family or friends to give you your space in this period. You do *not* have to entertain visitors. Have them over if you want, but don't feel obligated to even come out of your bedroom—or let them in—if you don't want to. Keep in mind that the brain is in a very unique state during this period. For some people, it is stressful just to have people lurking about. That's fine. These days and weeks are not about them. This time is all about you and your baby—taking care of mom so mom can take care of the baby.

Ideally, you will have people dropping by to drop off some food and do some chores. They may pop their head in your bedroom to take a peek at the baby, but do not feel obligated to play host to them—or even let them hold the baby—while you feel that way. There will be plenty of time for long chats and cuddles later, when you're out of that whirlwind stage.

Once you're comfortable with having people over, schedule visitors slowly and in a staggered manner so they don't all arrive on the same day and overwhelm you. Put yourself and your family first. Be confident about setting limits for the length of each visit. You're the parent, and you're in charge. If you're not comfortable dictating these rules, enlist your partner or a friend to be the gatekeeper. Designate a secret code word for when it's time to politely wrap up the visit.

Continue doing kangaroo care and encouraging the breast crawl as you are able. Feel free to warn visitors that they can visit the baby but you're not putting on a shirt.

NEWBORN CARE

It's normal for newborns to sleep for a couple of days after birth, then wake up and start to eat very frequently. Newborns will want to be fed every one to two hours in this stage, and at certain times of the day, you may be feeding almost constantly. Newborns do this because they're growing incredibly rapidly, and if you're breastfeeding, they're being instinctually driven to drive up your milk supply by constantly stimulating your breasts to make more milk. Isn't nature amazing?

Infant massage is another lovely practice that will help you bond with your baby and foster growth. This practice will be as relaxing for you as it is for baby, and you'll build a bond by focusing your attention entirely on your baby. This is also a wonderful bonding option for partners who may be struggling to find a way to feel useful.

Touch is an important need for babies, so while we normally think of massage as a luxury, this practice is not at all frivolous or unimportant. In fact, studies on infant massage have found that 10 to 15 minutes of touch every day reduces their levels of cortisol, a stress hormone. This reduction in cortisol allows for better absorption of nutrients, thereby increasing growth by significant, measurable amounts. Infant massage is most helpful right after the evening bath because it helps baby relax for sleep. Just don't expect the massage to consistently induce sleep in the immediate newborn period as it takes a while for babies to develop a normal diurnal sleep pattern after living in darkness for nine months.

BONDING IN THE NICU

During my pregnancy with Aram, I remember feeling worried that I wasn't going to bond with him. You see, Aram wasn't my first child. At the time Aram was born, I had an African serval, which is a majestic-looking cat that resembles a small cheetah.

His name was Obi, and I loved him so much. I couldn't imagine being bonded with my baby the way I was bonded with my cat. I remember everyone asking me, "But isn't it going to be dangerous to have this cat around the baby?" I was adamant that we would figure out a way to make it work so that I would never have to part with this cat.

When Aram came along, true to my fears, the feelings of bonding did not come immediately. To this day, I don't know if my feelings were normal or because of the birth trauma I had experienced or simply because he came early. But I carried on, settling into a routine of going into the NICU every day to breastfeed him. One day, a couple of weeks after his birth, I looked down at him in the NICU, and the bond kicked in. It didn't feel like anything in particular. I didn't feel any kind of hormone surge or anything like that. I just realized that my priorities had been rearranged, and I knew I needed to protect this child. And in that moment, I think I would have gladly thrown my cat under a bus to save my baby, without a second thought.

It may sound ridiculous that I was afraid that I would love my cat more than my baby, but hormones are ridiculous. When those parental instincts do kick in, it can feel weird, but that's okay. Parenting is trial by fire, even for the most organized among us.

ADOPTIVE BABYMOON

Every family will have a unique experience with adoption. Bringing my adopted son Samuel home was, as you might expect, a completely different experience than I had with Aram. In many ways, my attempts to attachment parent Samuel failed miserably—and hilariously.

First, since cosleeping is the norm in Ethiopia, we thought it might make Samuel feel more welcome to have him sleep in our bed with us, as Aram did. Samuel had a different plan. Cosleeping was not just normalized at the orphanage, it was necessary. And it had been very cramped. So, when he noticed that there was a bed waiting for him, he was excited. I'll discuss Samuel's cosleeping story more in Chapter 4.

Second, I wore Samuel everywhere. I don't know if it was instinctual or if it was something more external, but I just felt like he needed to be carried. Now, you might not think that that is very strange for an attachment parent, but Samuel was overweight because of the processed food at the orphanage, and I am very petite. He was so heavy. So much so, I gave myself back problems. And because of his size, my carrying him just looked ridiculous.

The process of bonding with Samuel was much slower than it was with Aram. For the first couple of months that I had Samuel, I kept looking at him and kind of thinking, "Who is this person? When is his mom going to come pick him up?"

But slowly, very slowly, through just going about the everyday business of caring for Samuel, I trained my brain to think of him as part of my "pack." And then, eventually, I trained myself to think, "This is my child." But this process was totally different than it was with Aram.

Sensitivity was key to helping Samuel adjust and to earning his trust. I learned that he had a strong need for control. For a brief period, if we'd tried to put on his clothes, he'd cry uncontrollably until he basically passed out. About a month after he came home, I made the mistake of giving him a haircut, not realizing that this triggered his anxiety, and he completely fell apart, making this deep sobbing sound, as if I had murdered someone. I felt terrible. But I learned to pay attention.

Overall, with Samuel, we got quite lucky when it came to his adjustment. Adoption really is, in most cases, a huge trauma for the child. Children are wounded, and they have special needs because of that. It is more common than not for adopted children to experience lasting behavioral issues precipitating from the transition. Samuel had had tantrums at the orphanage, and we were fully expecting more when he arrived home. But he had one or two, then it never happened again. I think the tantrums were largely related to his personality as to this day Samuel has a strong need for control and predictability in his life. I think that need is why he likes school so much these days.

I'd like to say that Samuel adjusted so well because of our attachment parenting or that it was because he came from a socially supportive, collectivist culture and had had a birth mother who deeply loved him but couldn't care for him. But with Samuel, I think we just got lucky in the genetics department. He was born with a very adaptable temperament. At the orphanage, Samuel was known for his amiable disposition—every single person who visited the orphanage remembered him. He's a really special kid.

But even though Samuel has a great disposition, the bonding process was still a challenge for us. In fact, I cannot remember a specific moment when everything clicked and our bond was solidified. My bonding with Samuel is more of an ongoing process that keeps evolving. With an adopted child, you begin the bonding process with a total stranger. You don't know her. And then you just build a relationship.

I think adoption bonding is easier with a baby, largely because you're doing everything you would otherwise be doing if you had given birth—lots of holding and possibly breastfeeding as well. And the brain is in a totally different developmental stage at that age, primed for forming attachments. But with a big kid, the situation is very different.

Adoption is not an easy road. The experience opened me up to a lot of things, and I feel very strongly that the focus should be on keeping families together whenever possible. Because adoption is unavoidably traumatic, it should be an absolute last resort, after all other options have been exhausted. If we, as a society, view the world as a Village and take responsibility for other people's children as if they were ours, there will not be as many orphans.

POSTPARTUM MENTAL ILLNESS

When Aram came home, I had been extremely ill and was suffering from PTSD. I remember feeling very confused because people kept trying to come over, and I had this tiny little preemie and didn't particularly want people near my baby at the time. I just wanted to focus on taking care of him.

The Searses (and many others) say to nap when the baby naps, and I tried to do that, but at that time, sleeping was hard for me. Because of where my head was at, the thought of falling asleep felt, for me, akin to dying. Life was heavy for me at that time, and I desperately wanted to escape reality. What I really enjoyed during this period was watching TV.

I am not actually a TV-watcher, but it's kind of hard to hold a book while you're breastfeeding, so breastfeeding and binge-watching became my life. I was suffering from PTSD and severe PPD, and at the same time, I was coming to realize that I was the only person who could take care of this helpless baby. So, TV became how I coped and how I comforted myself. I was resting, and I was always lying with my baby next to me on the bed, but at the same time I was escaping into a fantasy world.

I was afraid to admit to people that I was watching TV to escape reality because TV doesn't sound like a very healthy way to cope. But now I think that it's okay to do things that you wouldn't normally do if they help you get through that difficult time—hibernating, binge-watching, whatever it looks like for you. I just wanted to hold my baby and watch TV and not move. I didn't want any visitors, just my mom or my husband there to take care of me.

MENTAL HEALTH CHECK

If you suspect that you may be suffering from postpartum mental illness, please don't be afraid to ask for help. Issues such as PPD are very common—estimated to affect 15 percent of new mothers. PPD is also extremely treatable; however, if left untreated, it can persist for months or even years. It's important to note that not only birthing mothers, but partners and adoptive parents of all genders are at risk for postpartum mental health conditions.

These are some signs and symptoms of PPD:

- Depressed mood
- Severe mood swings, irritability, and anger
- Crying more than usual
- Reduced energy/fatigue
- Trouble emotionally bonding with baby
- Sleep difficulties
- Withdrawal from others
- Reduced interest in favorite activities
- Changes in appetite
- Hopelessness
- Shame, guilt, feeling like a bad parent
- Difficulty concentrating
- Anxiety
- Thoughts of harming yourself or your baby

Sometimes, when you're deep in the throes of a mental illness episode, the people around you can notice things you can't, which can make all the difference. It can be very helpful to enlist your close friends and family in monitoring you in the weeks and months after birth for signs that you may be suffering. Postpartum mental illness is usually diagnosed between two and four months postpartum. If you are having unsettling thoughts, please tell someone. Another mom that you trust is a great place to start. Chances are, she's had them, too. Whatever you do, please don't suffer in silence. Keep those lines of communication open.

If you need immediate help, please call the Suicide Prevention Helpline at 1-800-273-TALK.

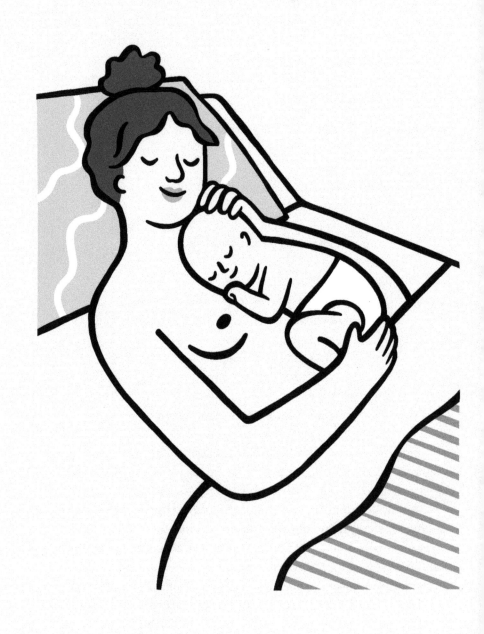

CHAPTER THREE

BREASTS, CHEST, OR SKIN: GIVE 'EM WHAT YOU'VE GOT!

Breastfeeding is a core component of attachment parenting. If you can't or couldn't breastfeed, don't skip this chapter. The inability to breastfeed is a huge reason families conclude that attachment parenting isn't for them, and I'm here to tell you: AP is totally for you. Regardless of what feeding looks like in your home, it is important to understand what breastfeeding really is (besides nutrition), how breastfeeding relates to attachment parenting, and how this understanding can help attachment parenting families who bottle feed.

First, let's get the basics out of the way. Breast milk is so much more than mere food. It contains over 200 ingredients, including, of course, what you normally think of as food, such as sugars, fats, and body-building proteins. But did you know that breast milk also contains enzymes that help break down fats and proteins into usable forms, and that it has special sugars that feed the baby's good gut bacteria? Beyond nutritive components, human milk also contains immune factors, including made-to-order antibodies, hormones that act as project managers and behavioral coaches, and even stem cells that scientists believe may help build crucial organ systems like the immune system, the endocrine system, and the brain.

Breast milk is more than food, and breastfeeding is about more than the milk. The hormones associated with lactation and feeding modify certain behaviors in both the parent and the infant. Prolactin is a mammalian hormone that, aside from driving milk production, is also associated with parental caregiving behavior in both biological males and females. Oxytocin, found in both the lactating parent and the nursling, produces an emotional feeling of closeness, and in the baby, oxytocin helps aid digestion and growth. Newer research suggests that the concentrations of melatonin and cortisol in the milk vary throughout the 24-hour day, possibly helping regulate the circadian rhythm of the baby and promote sleep development. Oxytocin and cortisol work in parents of both biological sexes to motivate them to respond to their babies when they cry, but the hormones are present in different concentrations in parents who breastfeed and breastsleep (a portmanteau of breastfeed and cosleep that was coined by anthropologists James McKenna and Lee Gettler, discussed in further detail in Chapter 4). We'll focus on these components when we talk about how to replicate some of the effects of breastfeeding if you're using a bottle. Many of these hormonal feedback systems are at least partially accessible to exclusively pumping and formula-feeding families.

If you wish to breastfeed, I encourage you to start your education in breastfeeding as soon as possible as there is a lot to learn. I've included some books on breastfeeding in the Resources section (page 117). I also recommend that you find a great lactation consultant in your area that you can call if you run into problems. Believe me, you don't want to search for a consultant when you're exhausted and sore from giving birth. Look for an International Board-Certified Lactation Consultant (IBCLC). This consultant has passed the most difficult exam that exists in lactation medicine and has received the highest level of training as well—even more than pediatricians get in this area. Ideally, you will meet the consultant or take a class before giving birth, but you will likely get a visit by a specialist during your hospital stay. Many lactation consultants will visit you at home, which is a godsend and absolutely worth it if you can afford it.

However, you may not be able to or not want to breastfeed, and that's okay. Regardless of what feeding looks like in your home, what I want you to know is this: You have the capacity for a deep, powerful, connection to your child. Science is just beginning to scratch the surface of how this connection works in both breastfeeding and non-breastfeeding parents. In this chapter, I invite you to stand with me on the cutting edge of this fascinating area of science. Take a deep breath and let's jump in.

FATHERS

Anthropologists Lee Gettler and Peter Gray have focused their research on fathers in some novel ways by studying fathers' hormones and behavior. They've found that dads who spend a lot of time with their kids—caring for them, cuddling with them, and all the everyday things—experience a dip in their testosterone over time and a rise in prolactin. Prolactin is a hormone found not just in lactating mothers but also in male primates who are involved with the care of their young. Researchers are unsure about why the testosterone dips, but it may be a signal to the father's body that it is no longer necessary to invest energy in finding a mate but to instead settle down and invest in his family. Beautiful, isn't it?

This biology is consistent with what we know of the psychological research on how attachment works in fathers. Fathers can be every bit as sensitive and attached to their children as are mothers—the attachment just happens through a slightly different mechanism. For women, the attachment forms through biologically carrying, and then caring for, the baby. For fathers whose partner is breastfeeding, the attachment is more about logging hours, and, therefore, may take a little time. Men build their attachment by spending time playing with their child and by participating in the day-to-day care—diaper changes, dressing, baths, and so on.

My simple advice for fathers and non-nursing partners is to stay involved every step of the way, to make mistakes, and to learn. There is no way to get good at anything except through practice. Be patient with the process and with yourself. You will be proud of and rewarded by your important role in your child's life.

ADOPTIVE PARENTS

A lot of people don't realize that adoptive parents can often breastfeed if they so choose. Similarly, if you breastfed your biological baby and weaned earlier than you wanted to and now you wish to continue, you can resume breastfeeding through a similar process. Contact an IBCLC to talk about the processes known as induced lactation (for adoption) or relactation (if you are seeking to resume breastfeeding after having stopped). They both usually involve taking a drug called domperidone and pumping regularly or putting baby to the breast to stimulate milk flow.

The parent and baby must also learn or relearn how to breastfeed. Because the tissue is already present, it is usually easier for parents, as well as babies, who have breastfed before to relearn how to breastfeed. Adoptive parents often use a supplemental nursing system (SNS), aids the process by providing more milk for him to pull than what the breast is producing alone. Results vary from family to family and are dependent on good support and dedication.

Allowing your baby to dry suckle is okay, too, if your baby finds it comforting. There are cultures in which non-lactating women, and even men, suckle others' babies because when you have a crying baby, you do whatever works. For most babies, the act of sucking means they're still hungry, but some babies may find comfort at your breast regardless of whether anything comes out. Note that dry suckling may induce lactation in some people, so don't attempt this if you're taking a medication that is not compatible with breastfeeding or have a medical condition that is aggravated by the hormones associated with breastfeeding. If you think that dry suckling is something you'd like to try, before introducing a pacifier, try allowing the baby access to your nipple instead. Do not try dry suckling if the baby is exhibiting strong hunger cues (see Chapter 5 for details) so he's not angry that nothing's coming out. You may have to try a few times or try different positions—just be patient. If it works for your baby, great. If not, I have a few other tricks up my sleeve for you.

OUR ADOPTIVE BREASTFEEDING STORY

For our family, adoptive breastfeeding was a wonderful, positive experience.

Having been breastfed by my mother until I was six, I was aware how important breastfeeding is to the child during a time of stress or trauma. Breastfed children do not normally use an inanimate item (such as a blanket or stuffed animal) to comfort themselves. They often use the closeness that breastfeeding provides from their mother.

So, not only was my child taken away from his homeland, culture, language, and family (most importantly, his mother), he was also stripped of the main action that provided him comfort.

Being able to breastfeed Samuel for almost a year was a beautiful experience. I wish I could say it was my idea. Truthfully, I thought he was too old to latch on to a new person for the first time. I was wrong!

Samuel had been curiously watching me breastfeed his brother (Aram was 2.5 years old at the time). He didn't speak English, but his curiosity conveyed that he was interested.

I spoke to Samuel's doctor, an MD who specialized in adoption, and he was extremely supportive of the idea to offer Samuel a spot nursing alongside his brother. His doctor was more concerned about my comfort level and alleviating any discomfort (due to cultural norms) that I had than whether breastfeeding should be offered. The answer to my question was simple: Yes, if I was comfortable, breastfeeding most definitely should be an available option for support.

At first, Samuel seemed too timid to ask outright. He was obviously afraid of being rejected when he showed the initial interest. When I asked him if he would also like to breastfeed, he smiled and jumped right on my lap. During our first experience breastfeeding, I could tell it was something he missed dearly—something from home that I was able to give him.

I am so happy I was able to provide him with the comfort he needed to get through trauma—trauma that most people will never experience in their entire life.

In our situation, Aram and Samuel got along great right away. But no matter how much we try to prepare ourselves for a new family member, the attachment process is not something logical. Attachment seems to happen at the most basic and biological level.

For us, we had this person in our home who felt new. And at almost four years old, Samuel was also a stranger whom we needed to get to know. Aram thought this new child was fantastic, but I don't think he truly grasped the idea that he was his brother or that I was the mother to both of them, until he realized that one of the most primal ways of seeking comfort and security was now also being offered to his playmate.

There were some other interesting observations we made about adoptive breastfeeding. For example, every Ethiopian I've encountered finds adoptive breastfeeding and extended breastfeeding to be completely normal. (Allonursing is still common in certain areas of the country.) One woman told me, "If there is milk, we use it." She went on to explain that breastfeeding eight-year-old children is not an uncommon practice. (And from a biological perspective, it is a normal length of time for our ape cousins, the orangutans.) And yet, due to lack of exposure and understanding of this basic biology, most Americans are horrified by it.

Adoptive breastfeeding definitely helped my attachment and bonding to my son, and it helped his attachment and bonding to me. Breastfeeding helped Aram understand Samuel's role in the family and see that Samuel was completely equal. I definitely think that there is great reason (sometimes even more so than with a biological child) to practice extended breastfeeding with an adopted child.

BREASTFEEDING IN THE NICU

In many cases, you can breastfeed your NICU baby. Certainly, pump your breast milk until baby can latch. In most cases, you should be able to practice kangaroo care (see page 25). In cases of jaundice, place a biliblanket underneath your baby, on your chest, and shine the standing lights on both mom and baby. You may need to negotiate with your doctors or nurses in order to be able to do this. Having regular consultations with a lactation consultant may help.

When you can breastfeed your baby, your doctor or nurse will need to measure baby before and after feedings in order to confirm how much baby is consuming. Any guesses or estimates could be very incorrect. Taking measurements is especially important if you are feeling pressured to supplement with formula, which is most likely to occur in the first few days after birth before your milk has come in. Pump after nursing to encourage your milk to come in more quickly.

If baby can't breastfeed for a long enough amount of time to get all she needs, you can use an SNS to give your baby more food—either formula or pumped breast milk—at the same time she is nursing, thus giving her more milk for less work. I really love Dr. Jack Newman's YouTube videos on how to use an SNS system.

Another option that may come in handy is a nipple shield. Nipple shields can be helpful if the baby has low muscle tone or is small because the shield can make breastfeeding easier. Nipple shields are also helpful if mom has inverted nipples or if a preemie has been bottle-nursed (formula or breast milk) and is resistant to switching to the breast. A device called LatchAssist Nipple Everter by Lansinoh can help prepare your nipple before breastfeeding and make it easier for your baby to latch. Similar results can be obtained by utilizing a pump for a few minutes before attempting to have baby latch.

Don't freak out too much about the long term or worry that breastfeeding with these tools might mean using a nipple shield or SNS for months or years. Most (if not all) babies will wean off of the breastfeeding assisting devices easily and quickly with assistance from a lactation consultant.

Also, keep in mind that incorrect latching doesn't apply only to the baby but to the pump as well. If it is uncomfortable to pump, you may have the wrong size breast shield. A lactation consultant, especially one who has experience with new mothers pumping in NICU, should be able to assist you with this.

Breastfeeding in the NICU can be really hard. I was sick, so physically getting to my baby was really challenging for me. My body just happened to make a lot of milk, but I can easily see how breastfeeding is difficult for so many NICU moms. Hats off to all of them, truly. Please remember that every little bit counts, and things will be so much better once you get home.

WHEN YOU'RE UNABLE TO BREASTFEED

Breastfeeding culture is complex, and I'm here to tell you that breastfeeding has nothing to do with ability to attachment parent. I have met many, many parents in my work, and I have yet to meet one that doesn't deeply, desperately love their child. Sometimes, though, all the love and dedication one heart can muster is not enough to overcome forces of biology, society, and politics that are outside of our control. For a bit of a deeper dive into the reasons why people often find themselves unable to breastfeed, see the section "Recognizing Why Many Parents Can't or Don't Breastfeed" on page 51.

When we hear about our friends' and family's struggles to breastfeed, our compassion for them compels us to say something to make it better. A popular thing to say is that, in the end, it doesn't matter how you feed your child, as long as your child is fed. It is a feel-good message that a lot of people who struggle with breastfeeding find comforting—at least, in an ephemeral sort of way. The tricky part is that it's not scientifically accurate.

Of course, it matters. Lactation is the defining feature of us mammals; we cannot just take it out of the equation and expect nothing to change.

You see, every animal, including humans, has an ecological niche—an ideal environment that helps them thrive. Environment is the first thing zookeepers think about when a zoo animal gets sick for mysterious reasons. The zookeeper looks at the animal's natural habitat and tries to recreate it as closely as possible. For human infants, who cannot move around their larger environment, their immediate environment constitutes a sort of micro-niche—that is, the parent's body, and in particular, the breastfeeding mother's body (though the father does some biological magic of his own—stay tuned). This is where the infants of our species and other primates spend most of their time, and it is the environment that shaped the evolved biology we have today. Breastfeeding is a fundamental component of that environment. But by attempting to recreate the baby's micro-environment, we can trick some parts of the baby's physiology into behaving and developing as if she is breastfed.

We've discussed how breastfeeding is nutritive as well as nurturing. Breastfeeding is nurturing primarily because of the behaviors associated with it. By understanding how breastfed babies and lactating mothers behave, we can better understand how to replicate those behaviors in our own way.

Sure, what you feed your baby matters, but what tools you use, how you hold your baby while you feed him, how you hold the bottle, and what you're paying attention to while you're feeding your baby are also important. Most of these factors you have control over, even if you're bottle feeding. The tricky part is many of these behaviors you attempt to replicate are nuanced and unconscious, driven by hormones. Replicating these behaviors will require a lot of mindfulness and a bit of extra effort without cortisol motivating you to respond to your baby and oxytocin to reward you for doing so. But the good news is these hormones are present in the brain of a non-lactating mother, and it's a positive feedback loop: The more you mimic these behaviors, the more active these hormonal systems will be.

RECOGNIZING WHY MANY PARENTS CAN'T OR DON'T BREASTFEED

You might have noticed that I'm not devoting a ton of real estate in this book to the breast vs. bottle debates that rage online. I think those debates focus on the wrong question. I'm not really interested in the question of whether parents should breastfeed their babies so much as I am concerned about what is stopping the ones who already want to. It is very important for both breastfeeding and formula-feeding families to understand these reasons so that breastfeeding families can have compassion for formula-feeding families and formula-feeding families can have compassion for themselves.

Parents have gotten the message about breastfeeding loud and clear, so the vast majority of parents start out wanting to breastfeed, and they go into birth planning to give it a whirl. Unfortunately, the vast majority end up cutting their breastfeeding journey shorter than they planned. According to the 2018 CDC Breastfeeding Report Card, 83.2 percent of families leave the hospital a breastfeeding family. And these are just the ones that felt confident and supported enough to even try. By three months, that number is nearly sliced in half—43.7 percent of those families have either introduced formula or switched to formula completely while their babies were still quite little. By the end of the first year, 56.85 percent of those families who had left the hospital wanting to breastfeed have switched completely over to formula. Although the drop-off does slow after the first few months, which are usually the roughest, that number is still a far cry from meeting the American Academy of Pediatrics' recommendation to breastfeed for a minimum of 12 months, and it's still further from the recommendation made by most other health organizations to breastfeed for a minimum of 24 months. If you struggled with breastfeeding, these numbers show that you're definitely not alone.

If many families start out wanting to breastfeed, what is stopping them? These numbers strongly suggest there are societal-level forces at play—that is, quitting breastfeeding is about more than individual choice. According to research by Marianne Neifert in 2001, the physical inability to breastfeed only accounts for 3 to 5 percent of cases where families stop breastfeeding; most causes are, ultimately, social. Social stigma, stress, incorrect information about how breastfeeding works, and subpar medical training are all factors that are fundamentally social in origin, and these factors can affect the biological process of milk production and the mother's perception of how much milk she is making.

The truth is that our society does not necessarily make it easy for families who want to breastfeed. In fact, in many ways, our society actively works to sabotage their efforts, especially for women in the workplace. Seasoned public health researchers will tell you that, "Individuals don't breastfeed; communities do." Let me explain what they mean by that.

It takes 8 to 12 weeks to hit a good groove with milk production, but the US is one of only two countries in the entire world that does not have a paid parental leave policy that would allow for this. (The other country is Papua New Guinea, if you were wondering.) Additionally, some medical professionals don't give the best advice or simply do not know how to diagnose and treat common breastfeeding challenges, so a lot of easily treatable problems get overlooked.

Perhaps most pervasively, though, our culture as a whole has forgotten how breastfeeding actually works, leading to a couple of generations of parents who don't really know what is normal, what a good latch looks like or how to achieve one, how to maintain supply, how breastfeeding affects normal infant sleep, or where to turn for help. To add insult to injury, public shame associated with this very basic, non-sexual, totally hygienic biological function can cause working moms to feel uncomfortable asking for time and space to pump, even though they're legally entitled to it, for fear of seeming uncommitted to their work.

You can see how the choice about whether to breastfeed your child, or for how long, is often not actually a choice at all—or, at least, it is not one freely chosen—for most families in the West. Whatever path led you here, know this: Regardless of breastfeeding status, the behavioral components of breastfeeding that help contribute to attachment are accessible to all families. It just takes a little self-education and special effort. So have compassion for yourself and your formula-feeding peers. We all face our own unique challenges. We're all just doing the best we can.

SKIN-TO-SKIN CONTACT

Breastfeeding meets a baby's strong neurological and emotional need for lots of close physical contact. One of the ways we can mimic this aspect of breastfeeding is through kangaroo care. Direct skin-to-skin contact allows for the flow of sensory information between the baby's body and the parent's body, which benefits them both. Many families do skin-to-skin in the early newborn period but don't do it as much as the baby gets older, particularly after weaning. I encourage you to continue this practice daily, during as many feeds as you can and during quiet moments, perhaps before bed. Kangaroo care is beneficial to baby, even when she is sleeping—particularly because it helps her to regulate her body temperature.

Think of your body as a kind of home for your child—a haven of emotional comfort, warmth, and safety. As baby grows, he will begin to venture farther away from home and perhaps stay away for increasing lengths of time, but he will always come home to ground himself.

When you are out and about, you can meet your baby's need for physical contact by holding him as much as possible. Babies don't just love to be held; they *need* to be held. For example, babies get held every time they breastfeed. A breastfed baby is naturally held more frequently than a baby fed with formula because breast milk is digested more quickly than formula, so the baby eats more frequently. Try to match the total amount of holding time throughout the day to the amount of time the baby would have spent breastfeeding. You can make this goal much more practical by wearing your baby in a sling, wrap, or supportive buckle carrier while you go about your daily activities. See Chapter 4 for more about the wonders of babywearing.

EVERY BIT COUNTS

Making time for skin-to-skin contact every day, responding quickly to your baby's cries, and holding her as much as a breastfed baby may sound daunting. Be kind to yourself. Remember that every little bit you can manage matters. Celebrate all your victories, large and small, and when you can't give everything you want, forgive yourself and move on, as many times as you need to.

BOTTLENURSING: A SPECIAL WAY TO FEED WITH A BOTTLE

When formula was first invented, bottle feeding was carried out with no real consideration for anything but the contents of the bottle and how much the baby consumed. No one really thought about how the delivery mechanism, not just the nutrition, changed. Specifically, bottle feeding affects how the baby is held, how quickly the milk flows, how often the feedings occur, and even what the baby and the caregiver are doing and thinking while they're engaged in this activity together. In this section, I am going to invite you to completely rethink the physical—and social—act of feeding baby.

You have different choices in terms of how you hold the baby and the bottle when you feed. Holding your baby during feeding is about more than just cuddling baby close and gazing lovingly into her eyes. The angle at which you hold the baby and the bottle determines how fast the milk flows, and it is this aspect, not nipple confusion, that is one of the key differences between breastfeeding and conventional bottle feeding. You can hold the baby and the bottle in such a way that requires more active participation on the part of the baby and lets the baby control the pace of the feed as she would control the flow of milk at the breast. Bottle feeding this way is a different experience for the baby, builds a different set of skills, and helps to prevent over-feeding. Letting baby control the pace of feeds is referred to by infant feeding professionals as *paced, responsive,* or *baby-led feeding*. The technique is the same whether there is formula or pumped milk in the bottle; only the preparation differs. I encourage you to check out the Resources section of this book (page 117) for more in-depth descriptions of paced feeding techniques.

These feeding techniques were developed mostly with breast-fed babies in mind—the goal being to help preserve baby's breastfeeding skills, while supplementing with bottles or while mom is at work, until breastfeeding could be resumed. My friend Bridget McGann, who, like me, has a background in anthropology and loves studying parent-infant behavior, is interested in incorporating the other behavioral components of breastfeeding with exclusively bottle feeding families in mind. She calls this new technique *bottlenursing*.

The term *bottlenursing* was coined separately from Bridget by Attachment Parenting International founders Barbara Nicholson and Lysa Parker with the same purpose in mind. Since then, paced feeding techniques have changed a little, and the social milieu of attachment parenting has changed a lot, but the concept is the same: bottle feed in a manner that is not just nutritive but also nurturing.

In this section, Bridget and I will give bottlenursing a bit of an update. Bottlenursing is distinctly different from conventional bottle feeding. Bottlenursing largely consists of paced feeding, but with a few added components and a more intuitive name. As we have discussed, breastfeeding activates a hormonal feedback system whereby a breastfeeding mother is chemically motivated to respond to her baby, chemically rewarded for having done so, and her brain is fine-tuned to become more responsive to her baby with practice. Through intensively responsive and high-contact care, fathers and non-lactating mothers experience their own hormonal changes that help them become more sensitive to their babies and tap into their own biological magic. At minimum, there is science to show that sensitivity and responsivity can be taught and improved with practice, but science has yet to discern the upper limits of what responsive, bottlenursing parents are capable of. So, let's just assume there are no limits!

Bottlenursing has five components: preparation, anticipation, bodies, bottles, and being present (time). As we go through the components, remember what we have discussed so far about the physiological needs that infants have, aside from pure nutrition, that breastfeeding helps meet: touch, eye contact, comfort, and warmth. Bottlenursing is where the behavioral research on breast-feeding really shines.

	CONVENTIONAL BOTTLE FEEDING	BOTTLENURSING
GEAR AND PREPARATION	• Focus is on the bottle design	• Focus is on how you use it
ANTICIPATION	• Watching the clock (schedule-driven) • Carer waits until baby cries to initiate the feed	• Watching the baby (cues-driven) • Carer begins bottle prep as soon as first cue is observed—or before, if you're expecting baby to become hungry soon!
BODY POSITIONING	• Baby is held lying down. • Body-contact is not considered. • Eye contact is not particularly encouraged past the new-born stage. • Baby is held on the same side for the full feed. • Older babies hold their own bottle.	• Baby is held sitting up or in a slight recline. • Baby may be held in a carrier or cuddled close so that "tummy-to-tummy" body-contact is allowed. • Face-to-face positioning may be used to encourage eye-contact and engagement. • Baby "switches sides" halfway through, just as with a breastfeed. • Baby is always held for a feed, for as long as a bottle is used.

BOTTLE POSITIONING	• Bottle is held upright so the liquid fully fills the bottle. • Liquid flows directly into back of baby's throat, forcing the baby to swallow whether or not they are hungry.	• Bottle is held roughly parallel to the ground so the liquid half-fills the nipple. • Baby must work to actively draw milk out of the nipple.
TIME	• Feed ends when bottle is empty. • Intake amounts are used to determine whether or not baby is "getting enough."	• Feed ends when baby stops sucking. • Satiation cues, developmental milestones, and weight gain are used to determine whether or not baby is "getting enough."

GEAR AND PREPARATION

You may be overwhelmed by how many kinds of bottles are available. Many are shaped like breasts in an attempt at biomimicry, but there isn't much evidence as to their effectiveness. Many people choose what is easiest to clean. Some bottle designs claim to prevent gas, but I'll debunk this myth. Gas is inevitable. No fancy-pants bottle is going to stop it. The key is not feeding too much or too fast. Even burping has, in recent years, been shown to be of questionable usefulness—especially at night. Please note: Babies with esophogeal reflux have a completely different protocol which you should discuss with your pediatrician.

One thing is imperative: Choose a nipple with a newborn flow and keep that flow as your baby grows. Ignore the advertising that encourages you to move up to greater flows. Recent research shows that it's not nipple confusion that we need to worry about so much as flow confusion.

Did you know that you also have a choice to use a cup or tube? Babies can, in fact, drink from a cup. There's a bit of a learning curve, but essentially, you hold a medicine cup to baby's lips so that the milk or formula barely touches his lips, and he sort of laps the milk up. An SNS is basically just a tube that allows you to supplement at the breast or feed the baby with your finger, which is called *finger feeding.* Finger feeding was originally conceived for babies with suckling issues or to avoid nipple confusion, but some people like this approach because it gives them more control and bodily contact with their baby. Both these methods engage babies actively in the feed, as they would be at the breast. In other words, if the babies don't actively suck, they don't get milk flow. This allows the babies complete control over the flow and gives their bodies adequate time to process the food.

ANTICIPATION

When a lactating mother hears her baby cry, neurotransmitters are stimulated in her brain, which tells the breast to release milk. This letdown sensation, coupled with a healthy little uptick in cortisol, motivates her to respond to her baby quickly—or she will need to change her shirt. This quick response by the mother's body benefits the baby by keeping the baby from spending too much time in a state of stress.

Even better, though, and more of an attachment parent reaction, is to anticipate a feed, and watch your baby for body language and noises that indicate hunger. A bottlenursing parent can then start preparing the bottle ahead of time, before the baby gets too worked up. Because it is important to boil the water for mixing formula, bottlenursing families need to pay close attention to baby for the earliest signs of hunger, so there is no huge rush. You want to watch baby for stirring at the end of a nap, followed by mouth-oriented behaviors, such as opening the mouth and sticking out the tongue, and bringing her hand up to her mouth. In Chapter 5, I go into more detail about how to read the special body language of babies.

Now that you're ready to feed, it's time to think about bodies, bottles, and being present (time).

NIGHTTIME FEEDING TIPS FOR BOTTLENURSING

Formula is safe and nutritious. However, all public health authorities stress that, despite widespread practices, powdered formula needs to be sterilized with boiled water. The water should hit the powder at a temperature of 158 degrees Fahrenheit (70 degrees Celsius) to kill any bacteria that could be lurking in the powder or in the nooks and crannies on the inside of the bottle. The formula should cool to at least body temperature (98.6 degrees Fahrenheit) before serving. Be sure to read the formula label for clarity on preparation.

All that prep time makes responding to baby quickly at night a bit trickier. The amount of sleep you get at night isn't about only how often baby wakes up but also how long it takes you both to get back to sleep. Less crying means a faster return to sleep. Here are a few tips to make things go more smoothly.

Stay one step ahead of baby: Learn to read baby's early hunger cues, sleep close to baby, and watch baby's routines so that you can grab a bottle before the baby escalates to a full screaming cry. If you can do this, baby will learn that there is no need to get worked up because help is coming. A baby that is less worked up will fall back asleep faster.

Dream feeding (level up): It is important to watch your baby, not the clock. Some babies, if we're lucky, keep a pretty steady routine. If you watch baby's routine very closely and time things just right, you can use a silent alarm to wake up right before baby usually does and initiate a feed while baby is still half asleep. The key is to feed your baby where they're sleeping, either as they're falling asleep or before they wake up.

Hot/cold hack: This mini refrigerator and bottle warmer combo can be a lifesaver at night. Put a mini refrigerator or cooler in your bedroom, upstairs hallway, or bathroom. Then put a bottle warmer in your bedroom or in the hallway just outside the door. Choose the quietest bottle warmer you can find—that is, one that won't wake the baby with a loud alarm. Before bed, prepare a night's worth of bottles with boiled water and pop them in your mini refrigerator. You will be grateful not to have to shuffle downstairs with a crying baby in your arms. Pre-prepared bottles of formula can be stored in the refrigerator for up to 24 hours if necessary.

BODIES: HOLDING AND POSITIONING

In addition to providing nutrition, breastfeeding is an interaction between two bodies, involving the transfer of body heat and gaze. And so, just as it's important to think about positioning while breastfeeding, it makes sense to think about positioning while bottlenursing.

Here is where we come to our first dramatic change from the traditional teachings about how to bottle feed. Traditional bottle feeding teachings dictate that babies be held in a cradle position for feeding. For bottlenursing, you sit the baby upright—yes, all the way up. You can let him recline a little, but you're aiming for a position that's more sitting than lying. You will notice immediately that, in this position, you are almost completely unable to tilt the bottle back. This is by design, and I'll explain why in a moment, when we talk about the bottle itself. Sitting the baby up also has the happy side effect of helping minimize acid reflux.

Baby is sitting up, but which way does he face? With breast-feeding, the baby is tummy-to-tummy with the mother. This fosters temperature regulation and gives the baby full view of his mother's face. With conventional bottle feeding, the bottle doesn't allow for full tummy-to-tummy contact, so we have to

modify the position a bit. Allow your baby to face perpendicular to your body and hug him close.

You may also sit with baby facing you, away from your body a bit, so you can talk or sing to him. Or, if you're sitting on a couch or the floor, you can bend your legs, bringing your knees up toward your chest, and prop the baby up on your thighs in front of you. This way, the baby's head is resting on your knees and his feet on your stomach, so you're face-to-face. This position will allow a freer use of one hand for play or a loving touch. As long as the baby is getting physical cuddling and eye contact, you've got the right idea: connection!

Just as a breastfeeding baby switches sides halfway through the feed, so, too, will you want to switch the baby from one side of your lap to the other and switch the hand that is holding the bottle. Switching sides helps build symmetrical body strength and hand-eye coordination, and some evidence shows that it helps strengthen the muscles in the eyes symmetrically, thereby preventing certain eyesight issues.

Another way to get that full tummy-to-tummy contact is to wear your baby during a feed. First, make sure she is already used to being worn. Newborns will take to it pretty much immediately, but older babies may resist when they're fussy. Once the baby is used to being worn, it helps to wear the baby to calm her while you prepare the bottle.

To feed the baby in a carrier, she will need to be in an upright position, tummy-to-tummy with you, and will need to turn her head to the side. Note that this feeding position should not be

used with babies who are under three months, and works better with bottles that are thinner, as opposed to the big, round, breast-shaped bottles. You may wish to loosen the top of the carrier a bit to allow the baby to recline a little—let her recline to the side, not out and away from your body. Grab a small washcloth or a tiny terrycloth bib to

catch dribbles before they land on your shirt or the carrier. Roll the cloth up and stick it under the baby's chin. Hold the bottle as level with the ground as you can and as close to your body as you can. Move around a little—don't bounce but sway a little or slow walk. Most little babies will fall asleep during the feed this way.

BOTTLES

One of the differences between breastfeeding and bottle feeding is that bottle-fed babies can get overfed—even if there is breast milk in the bottle. When you bottle feed in the conventional manner, with baby lying flat, gravity causes the milk to flow directly into the back of the baby's mouth with very little effort, and the baby has no choice but to swallow or choke. In fact, the choking risk associated with the continuous flow of an up-tilted bottle is the primary reason bottlenursing parents are urged never to prop up the bottle.

You're not just a bottle holder, though. You serve an important, active role in feeding your baby. And the baby is active, too. During breastfeeding, the baby must extract the milk, which takes a lot of work. With a bottle, you can engage the baby in the activity by only giving him milk when he is actively sucking. You'll achieve this by holding the bottle at a lower angle so the baby must actively draw the liquid out. The bottle should be level with the ground, and the nipple should be about half filled with liquid.

But what about bubbles? Once again, gas is something we really can't do much about. Worrying about bubbles in the formula is an antiquated concern because even if you cannot see any bubbles, microscopic air bubbles are still present. Instead, let's focus on the variables we can control.

As babies grow, they develop the ability to hold a bottle on their own. However, I encourage you to continue to hold the bottle anyway, if you can. When babies hold their own bottles, they tend to wander. Of course, that is not an option if the baby is breastfeeding. A breastfed baby learns that, if you want to feed, you must come to your mom, lie still, and be present. This lays the foundation for skills in emotional regulation, self-control, and mindfulness. Isn't it good to know that these beautiful evolutionary behaviors can also be successfully translated into your bottlenursing activities?

BEING PRESENT (TIME)

Breastfeeding teaches parents a little mindfulness, too. As you read this, you may have noticed that this approach to feeding a baby takes a little longer than the traditional approach to bottle feeding. This is by design as well. Breastfeeding parents often talk about how breastfeeding by nature forces you to stop now and again throughout the day, sit down, and smell the proverbial roses. Having to stop what you're doing can be inconvenient, of course, but breastfeeding moms also describe it as one of the more surprising and positive aspects of breastfeeding, which is why the final component to bottlenursing is time—we'll call it *being present* simply because it's easier to remember along with *body* and *bottle.*

First, it is important for growth—and likely for many other reasons scientists have yet to uncover—to feed all babies on demand, which means watching the baby for hunger cues (discussed in Chapter 5) and feeding when baby is hungry. Baby will communicate to you when it is time to feed, and this timing varies from baby to baby, from day to day, and even from hour to hour. This is normal human behavioral variation.

It can be hard for us to accept this variation when we live in a culture where parenting is becoming increasingly data-driven, with a new app dropping every day for tracking behaviors and bodily functions. It is hard to resist that need for control. But it may help to think of it this way: There are plenty of things in child development that we do not micromanage, such as the rate at which our child's hair grows, which grammar rules they have deciphered, or how long it has been since they last sang a nursery rhyme. We simply trust that all these things will naturally happen with very little conscious interference from us. As the saying goes, "Watch your baby, not the clock."

During the feeding itself, many babies will take little breaks and stop sucking for a few breaths. This is true for both breastfed and bottle-fed babies. Watch your baby while she eats, and when she stops actively sucking, tilt the bottle down so the liquid flows out of the nipple. If you listen to the baby's breathing in these moments, it might sound like she's taking a little breather because sucking is hard work. Wait until she resumes sucking again, then tilt the bottle back up so the liquid flows back into the nipple.

Cultural conditioning and busy lives may tempt us to try to force the baby to finish the bottle, but try to resist the urge. Instead, follow the baby's appetite. It's hard, I know. We've been taught to finish eating all our food for generations now. Following the baby's appetite will mean shorter, more frequent feeds. Again, shorter, frequent feeding is how a breastfed baby feeds, and it's how your bottlenursed baby can feed, too. Let your baby be your guide to whether he's getting enough. A fed newborn baby will become sleepy or relaxed as he becomes full. And in general, as the baby grows, he will become relaxed but not necessarily fall asleep. Pumped milk can be safely put back in the fridge for up to two hours and used for the next feed.

You'll want to make the most of this time together. To pass the time during a feeding, talk or sing to your baby. One of the aspects of breastfeeding that developmental psychologists find most interesting is the face-to-face interaction it encourages. Babies love these little interactions, and it also fosters brain development.

But at the same time, understand that even breastfeeding parents don't sit around gazing lovingly into their babies' eyes every

second of every feed. They may spend feeds chatting with people around them, entertaining a toddler, and, yes, "brexting." Try to take baby out and about to relieve the boredom. Breastfeeding is an intensely social behavior, and bottlenursing can be, too.

Finally, spend time with breastfeeding families. As discussed, many of the hallmark breastfeeding behaviors are nuanced, unconscious, and difficult to describe. A wonderful way to learn them and figure out how to integrate them into your bottlenursing approach is by being around breastfeeding. A lot of these suggestions also tend to be somewhat countercultural, and you may find that the exposure helps normalize them for you. If you don't have any friends who are currently breastfeeding, check out your local La Leche League group.

I hope you find bottlenursing to be a helpful and empowering tool. It will not completely close the gap between formula feeding and the advantages afforded to babies by breastfeeding. Breastfeeding is a wondrously complex biological system that scientists have barely even begun to understand, let alone be able to recreate artificially, and there are profound effects that simply cannot be explained by behavior alone. Rather, my hope is that bottlenursing becomes a way by which formula-feeding families can rewrite their own narratives about what sort of parents they are and want to be, and what they are capable of. I also hope that bottlenursing is a way for them to feel included in the attachment parenting community. Attachment parenting belongs to everyone, regardless of circumstances.

BREASTFEEDING AND MEDICATION

The most common concern about contraindications to breastfeeding is medications for postpartum anxiety, depression, and psychosis. Many new moms were not on psychoactive drugs before having a baby, and they become worried about the effects the drug might have on their breastfeeding baby. Rest assured, most drugs given to mothers for postpartum mental illness enter the breast milk in either very small or undetectable amounts and are compatible with breastfeeding. Unfortunately, many parents are told to wean their babies when starting a medication, only to later find out that the medication was, in fact, compatible with breastfeeding.

When considering whether a medication is compatible with breastfeeding, it is important to work with an IBCLC in concert with your prescribing doctor. This is because most physicians, including obstetricians, are not adequately trained in breastfeeding and medicine. An IBCLC is the most highly trained specialist you can find in this area of expertise.

Many attachment parents are often averse to taking a psychotropic medication, even if trusted medical institutions have judged them to be safe. Some feel these medications are unnatural or toxic. Others feel like taking medication is admission of failure and think they should try exercise or meditation first.

It's difficult to trust products made by companies that insist on airing two-minute commercials for drugs to treat erectile dysfunction while we're trying to feed the kids dinner. I think, though, it is important to remember that chronic stress can be toxic in and of itself. Although scientists are still studying how stress hormones like cortisol, which is present in breast milk, act in the body of the nursling, we can at least say that chronic stress causes damage in the mother's body, affecting everything from her cancer risk to her memory and accelerating the aging process. I don't say this to stress you out even more. I just want you to know that toxicity comes in many forms, and there is a trade-off to forcing yourself to endure unnecessary suffering.

Yes, there is compelling evidence that exercise and meditation can help with depression and anxiety. Most of that research, however, is on the general population, and very little evidence exists to support any effect for postpartum mood and anxiety disorders. Moreover, in these studies on the general population, to get the desired effect, these activities must be performed every day. In the case of meditation, there is a dose-response effect, with most studies starting with a minimum of 20 minutes of mindfulness-style meditation every day.

Sometimes, however, these alternative approaches are not quite enough, and that is okay. Needing help is not an admission of failure or inadequacy, and it's not selfish. Self-care is not "me instead"—it's "me, too." Exercise, meditation, and eating lots of vegetables and fruit are all going to be helpful and work wonderfully alongside medication. Most women only need to be on medication temporarily.

If nothing else, keep the lines of communication open with a qualified psychologist and ask questions. Remember, no one can force you to initiate a treatment that you are not comfortable with. Even if you start a medication, you are free to change your mind at any time.

At minimum, if you are suffering from a postpartum mental illness, see a therapist regularly, so you have somebody keeping tabs on you.

An authoritative scientific resource for medication and breastfeeding compatibility is LactMed, a database maintained by the National Institutes of Health (see Resources, page 117). I also highly recommend following the Lactation Pharmacist on Facebook.

CHAPTER FOUR

BABYWEARING AND BEDROOM SHARING

BABYWEARING

For nine months in the womb, baby was held continuously, without ever being put down. He enjoyed constant warmth and motion and the steady, unceasing *whoosh-whoosh* of his mom's blood rushing through her descending aorta, located right next to his ear. It makes sense then that cuddling, rocking, bouncing, and white noise will continue to soothe baby once he's born.

Science supports the importance of being held. Evidence shows that being held maximizes the calorie efficiency for both the infant and the person carrying the baby which supports optimal infant growth. Babies who are held are calmer and learn more readily. They cry less. Their baseline cortisol (stress hormone) is lower. Physical therapists believe that being held supports the healthy development of the hips and lumbar curve (the small of your back) for walking. Since it takes pressure off the skull and engages the infant's core strength and neck control, holding your baby eliminates the need for "tummy time"—an invention of the West that was necessitated by the practice of leaving babies lying on their backs for long periods of time, leading to plagiocephaly, or flat head syndrome. Holding babies also affords them easy access to their two favorite things: breasts and faces.

We've talked about breasts. Let's talk about faces for a moment. Baby brains come pre-wired to stare at faces and face-like shapes because, as humans evolved to be more intensely social, reading faces became crucial to survival. For us adults, it is second nature. This is the literal, actual explanation behind the myth of the man in the moon and why so many people tend to see Elvis in a piece of toast. Seeing faces is a quirk of human psychology. Beyond seeing faces, however, reading faces is a highly nuanced and difficult skill to learn. To catch on, babies must spend a lot of time people watching and interacting.

Babies' interest in faces is one reason babies are captivated by peek-a-boo. Being held brings babies up to face level, where they have more faces to look at. They love this, and looking at faces is good for their development because it lays the neurological foundations for perspective taking, empathy, theory of mind, and all the skills that will ultimately help them build relationships.

As Paul Eckman discussed extensively in his book *Emotions Revealed: Recognizing Faces and Feelings to Improve Communication and Emotional Life*, studying faces is the beginning of the skills they'll use to navigate a socially complex world, from reading the subtle body language of a teammate on the soccer team to gauging whether a joke will land well before they make it.

Babywearing is basically an avenue for making holding more convenient and easier on the biceps. While baby carriers may seem like a pretty contemporary concept, they are thought to be one of the earliest tools humans invented, dating anywhere from 50,000 years ago to possibly millions of years ago. We can't be exactly sure when carriers were developed because they would have been made from animal skins or fibrous netting, which would decay quickly and not turn up in archaeological records. Near-constant carrying is virtually universal for primate infants, as is a stress response when baby is separated from the mother. The invention of the baby carrier was practical as it meets baby's intense and constant need for physical contact and protection while also allowing us to go about our business as adults.

Babywearing is ubiquitous in indigenous cultures the world over, and there are a wide variety of carrier styles and construction. Many types of carriers are available in stores these days, and almost every major city in the Western world has an educational group whose members will enthusiastically share their insights on how to use them most effectively (see Resources, page 117).

Happily, most people can babywear. Many parents with physical disabilities, for example, find baby carriers to be a crucial adaptive tool for parenting. The key is to get the right carrier for you. They're all engineered differently. For example, some carriers work better for people with narrow shoulders, and others fit better on people with wide shoulders. Larger people often choose to buy a longer wrap or a buckle extension. If there's a local babywearing group or store in your area, talk to them to get help. Try a lot of carriers on before you buy one.

Sometimes, babywearing is prohibitive, usually for the same sorts of reasons that restrict the ability to hold your baby, such as back pain or balance issues that make babywearing an unsafe choice. In these cases, your go-to AP strategies will include alternate kinds of touch and help from other adults.

Touch comes naturally to most parents, so they don't have to really think about it. But if your baby cannot be held by you, you may need to consciously remind yourself to touch your baby throughout the day to meet her need for physical contact. Any time of day is a great time to stroke your baby's arm, back, or head. Infant massage is another handy tool for meeting your baby's need for contact. There are instructions all over the internet and in attachment parenting books for how to do infant massage.

Don't be afraid to enlist the help of other adults in your circle—preferably those who are familiar to your baby and will be in their lives in the long term. Most people are more than happy to hold a baby. In the early months, babies are well adapted to be held by multiple people, not just their parents, throughout the day. But as they grow, babies often go through phases in which they cling more to mom or dad, which is completely normal and healthy. These stages can be challenging, but don't allow yourself to feel guilty about any physical limitations—instead, capitalize on all the wonderful attachment tools you do have to give, whether that's face time, massage, nursing, cosleeping, or cuddling.

When you are separated for a long period and unable to hold your baby for hours, days, and weeks on end, both you and your baby yearn for closeness. Babywearing is a wonderful act to achieve closeness and comfort without overstimulating your baby. For babies born prematurely, you want to create as much of a warm and comfortable womb-like experience as possible, which is why babywearing is so wonderful.

BABYWEARING SAFETY TIPS

There are several important components of safe babywearing. Often presented in a form of a checklist, there are different acronyms that are used to aid parents with memory. The most popular one is "**TICKS**," but my friend Bridget has found that it is not particularly intuitive, so she has developed this one, "**THICK**."

Tight: This one should really be "snug" but "**SHICK**" is a very non-sensical acronym! Babies like to be snug and secure, because that is what they were in the womb! Obviously, you don't want to squeeze the living daylights out of your baby, but the point here is that baby's back needs to be well-supported in order to keep her from falling out of the carrier when you bend over. But baby will feel safer, too. Many parents are afraid, at first, of tightening their carrier as much as babies like it to be. But the next three letters in this acronym will help you monitor your baby's breathing, and you will know how tight is just tight enough!

High: Baby should be held high so you can closely monitor their breathing. When held in front, they should be "close enough to kiss" without having to bow your head down too far. When doing a back carry, your baby's head should be level with the nape of your neck, so you can feel them breathing on the back of your neck, and baby can peek over your shoulder while awake.

In view: Look to make sure you can see your baby's face at all times. This ensures adequate airflow and breathing.

Chin off chest: If baby's head is bent too far forward, their airway can be compressed, causing "positional asphyxia." This is the cause of many babywearing-related deaths (usually when baby is carried in the cradle position in poorly-designed sling-style carriers) and is the reason that the first step in infant CPR is to tilt the head back to open the airway. To keep baby's airway open during babywearing, you want their chin to be up off their chest so their head is more or less in line with their spine, or even tilted back a little.

Knees higher than butt: Legs in an "M" or "frog leg" position with knees high, with fabric spread from knee to knee ensures that the baby's center of gravity is cradled like a hammock. This creates a "deep seat" that makes it harder for babies to slide or pop out of.

Bridget encourages parents to use their hands to run through their checklist. Using your hands helps commit the acronym to memory. Run your hands over the part of your baby related to each letter, in order, to associate each letter with a physical movement—**(T)**ight: Back of baby (to check back support), and front of baby (to check the space between bodies), **(H)**igh: Kiss top of baby's head, **(I)**n view: Touch baby's face, **(C)**hin off chest: Touch baby's chin, **(K)**nees higher than butt: Run fingers from knee to knee.

Additionally, always keep one hand—and one half of your brain—on baby at all times. Babywearing is an assistive tool, not a replacement for your own mindfulness and touch. Have a backup plan, such as a stroller or another adult, to replace babywearing when you are inebriated, injured, or overtired.

BABYWEARING A PREEMIE

When Aram was born, I was excited just to have him home and hold him. When he was a preemie, I wore him in a Moby Wrap because I felt like it was womb-like. When he got bigger, I put him in an Ergo. I would breastfeed him in it and wear him while I did chores.

Preemies can get easily overstimulated by the outside world because they're not supposed to be out in it yet. I love babywearing because it helps recreate that womb-like experience for preemies. You can use pieces of fabric to block the light, and the closeness makes babies feel safe and secure. Babywearing can also help you monitor a preemie very closely and keep her stimulated just enough.

Around the time you can begin skin-to-skin contact, start talking to your baby's nurse about any special modifications you might need to make for your baby. Since preemies are susceptible to positional asphyxia, pay close attention to the babywearing safety rules for keeping the baby's chin off their chest and keeping the airway open.

For the most part, wearing a preemie or a baby who is small for gestational age is the same as wearing a bigger baby, but you want to choose a carrier that is more fabric-based, that is thin, soft, and customizable. Start researching carriers as soon as you know or suspect your baby will be arriving early. Try to visit one of your local babywearing groups, as they often have libraries of different carriers you can try on. Trying on different carriers is immensely helpful because baby carriers are basically functional clothing. But it's okay if you don't have time to do this right away because a stretchy wrap like the Moby Wrap works great for most preemies. And with a little clever wrapping, the carrier can also accommodate tubes and wires. A very broken-in ring sling will be a great carrier once they're ready to go home because the slings are very soft and pliable. Ring slings are also easy to get on and off, which makes them great for quick errands and for using around the house.

COSLEEPING

Until about 200 years ago, shared sleep was a human universal. Cosleeping is colloquially conflated with bed sharing, but in fact, cosleeping is an umbrella term. Bed sharing is just one form of cosleeping. Cosleeping encompasses any situation in which a baby or child sleeps "within sensory range" of a caregiver. Baby may be in the same room but on a separate surface, or he may be on the same surface. The world over, babies sleep on mattresses with their parents, in cradles, in little swings, on mats on the floor, in a hammock with mom or dad, on a futon with mom, or in a papoose strung from the ceiling. Cosleeping is shared sleep, as humans have always done, and as many still do.

A little-known fact is that cosleeping in the general sense is recommended by every major pediatric medical organization in the world. Cosleeping has been shown to reduce risk of unexplained infant death and sudden infant death syndrome (SIDS) by two to three times. For this reason, the American Academy of Pediatrics recommends that babies sleep in the same room as their primary caregivers for the full first year to prevent SIDS and to support breastfeeding. Where the American Academy of Pediatrics stands alone from the rest of the world is in its stance against bed sharing. Citing risks of suffocation and a belief that bed sharing increases the risk of SIDS, the organization recommends against it. For information on the safety of bed sharing, I recommend reading James McKenna's *Safe Infant Sleep: Expert Answers to Your Cosleeping Questions.*

I often find that parents don't like that the American Academy of Pediatrics recommends having the baby sleep in their room for a full year. Many parents move the baby out of their room way earlier because they say that the baby sleeps better that way. I think what some parents don't realize is that what makes cosleeping protective against SIDS is that it keeps babies from spending too much time in a deep state of sleep from which it's difficult for them to come out of. As a society, we misunderstand normal human infant sleep—it's supposed to be light and fragmented. You don't want babies sleeping too long or too deeply because for some babies, in rare circumstances that we can't always predict, deep sleep might be dangerous.

Both parents and infants tend to have a strong instinctual drive to be close to one another at night, which drives parents to bring their babies into bed regardless of what authorities tell them. Broad, sweeping, one-size-fits-all condemnations of a practice with no exceptions, qualifiers, or explanations generally don't make for effective health policy, but it is important to note that anthropologist James McKenna, found that only breastfeeding mothers should share a sleep surface with their baby, as non-lactating moms lack the instinctive awareness to prevent them from rolling onto the baby. This strong instinctual drive to sleep close to each other is higher in breastfeeding dyads, so as breastfeeding rates continue to go up (we hope), so will bed sharing. In the interest of informed decision-making, then, health authorities are better off taking a more comprehensive approach to parent education—comprehensive sleep education.

Cosleeping, safely practiced in all its forms, meets both the baby's and the nursing mother's strong drive for proximity to one another. This proximity drive does not clock out at night, and it has evolved alongside breastfeeding. Sleep is so inextricably tied to breastfeeding that anthropologist James McKenna created the term *breastsleeping* to describe how neither breastfeeding nor sleep can be fully understood without also exploring the other.

One of the most difficult things to deal with in attachment parenting is what to say to bottle feeding parents who feed their baby in the on-demand, baby-led way that we discussed in Chapter 3 and who feel a strong instinct to bed-share but are afraid of the risks. Indeed, bed sharing is not recommended outside of an exclusively breastfeeding relationship. The reason for this is because the sleep structure—that is, the brainwaves—of a bed sharing dyad (mom and baby) is fundamentally different than that of a dyad that does not sleep together. If mom is breastfeeding and sleeping with her baby, their waking, activity, breathing, and heart rate synchronize. Also, babies who are breastfed orient themselves toward the breast because that is where their food comes from, and they are therefore less likely to fall out of bed.

To summarize: Cosleeping, in some form, is recommended by every major medical organization in the world. Bed sharing, colloquially referred to as cosleeping, is only recommended for exclusively breastfed babies.

Rest assured, though, that if you room-share but don't bed-share, you are still cosleeping. And you and your baby derive many benefits from this happy medium. Primarily, you will become attuned to your baby and be able to respond to her cries quickly at night. And baby gets attuned to your presence, too. When your baby doesn't have to wait for you to hear her cry and shuffle down the hall to her room, she has less time to get worked up. Just like any child or adult, the more a baby gets worked up, the harder it is for them to settle down.

In fact, you may become so synchronized with your baby's sleeping and waking patterns that you start to wake before your baby when it's time to feed. If you have learned to read your baby's cues, you'll know when a little grunt or squirm means hunger, and you will be able to prepare a bottle before baby wakes up, feed her while she's still half asleep, and settle her back down again without much fuss.

Cosleeping changes as babies get older. Remember, a toddler bed in your bedroom is still cosleeping. We got our kids a bed in their own room and just let them crawl back into our bed whenever they wanted, so that the transition was gradual. Like many areas of development, it's kind of a "take two steps forward, one step back" process. I think this helped keep the transition from becoming an issue. You can let your kids pick out their own bedding to make it more exciting for them.

There are many same-room setup options. Let's explore a few:

Sidecar bassinet: This popular option attaches to the side of your bed but has a barrier to keep the baby from rolling onto the adult mattress. A sidecar bassinet, such as the Arms Reach Co-sleeper, allows you to meet your baby's need for contact by reaching over and placing a hand on him or patting him to sleep. Some people simply remove one side of their crib and sidecar it to the parent bed using straps. This attachment must be done tightly so there is zero gap between the mattresses for baby to fall into. There are many online resources for how to attach the crib. To keep the baby from rolling onto your bed, one popular hack is to place a pool noodle under the crib sheet on the open side. Duct tape it to the mattress to keep it in place.

Standard crib or bassinet: Many families simply place a crib or bassinet in the parent's bedroom. If the master bedroom is small, some families remove dressers and other items from the master bedroom to make room for a crib and turn a spare bedroom (or what otherwise might be a nursery) into a sort of walk-in closet.

Toddler bed or mattress on the floor: A toddler bed is low to the floor, and some cushioning below the bed can help protect against injury if the little one falls out. Puzzle mats for playrooms are great for this protective cushioning, but be creative. Babies really can just sleep on a mattress on the floor if you babyproof the rest of the room. There's nothing special about a crib other than that it keeps the baby contained. You can use the pool noodle trick to keep baby from rolling off the mattress.

Adult bed in nursery: Another option is to place an adult twin bed in the baby's nursery.

The bottom line is that there is not just one way to set up your family sleeping arrangement. Take time to consider what works best for you.

COSLEEPING WITH AN ADOPTED CHILD

Adoptive cosleeping can help the child feel safe and secure. For older children, cosleeping should be offered as an option, but never forced.

Samuel came to us from a culture where cosleeping was normalized, and it was necessary at the cramped orphanage. So, we began by cosleeping with him because we thought it might make him feel more at home and because it was what Aram was doing. Samuel had a different plan.

Samuel didn't speak English, but we could tell that he was curious about the toddler bed that we had and that he was wondering whose it was. When we told him that it was his, his eyes lit up with excitement. We realized that because, in Ethiopian culture, sleep is shared socially and because there was never any fear or tension surrounding sleep in the early years, he—now four years old—was ready to sleep in his own bed. But also, since cosleeping is so normalized in his culture, it was boring for him. He had never had his own bed before. In his birth home, Samuel slept with his entire family on a bed that fit wall to wall in their communal bedroom. He was accustomed to a very cramped sleeping experience. The idea of having his own bed was an exciting new thing. After that, Samuel slept in his own bed, and soon Aram would often sleep with him. We think cosleeping helped solidify their brotherly bond.

CHAPTER FIVE

BIRDS CHIRP, BABIES CRY

When we are born, the first thing we learn is how to ask for help with a big, loud cry. This behavior is nothing short of revolutionary because it's baby's first lesson in a crucial human skill: communication. When the Searses speak of belief in baby's cries, they're basically talking about maximizing communication efficiency between baby and parent. The two parental behaviors found to be most strongly associated with a secure attachment are sensitivity, which means accuracy in identifying the child's need, and responsivity, which is consistently and actively meeting that need. By *actively*, I mean either anticipating the need before the child signals it or responding as quickly as possible once the baby signals. Don't worry—literally no one responds quickly and accurately 100 percent of the time, and responding is a skill that you get better at with practice.

Babies also communicate their needs through a variety of vocalizations and a universal body language. Your job as a parent is to crack the code, identify the need, and send a message back by meeting that need. If you respond consistently and accurately, your baby learns which kind of signals consistently get the most accurate results, and her skills in communicating her needs become more refined. Your accuracy in responding increases, as does her accuracy in signaling. The harmony that results is the beginning of a secure attachment. Your baby begins to learn that she can trust you to meet her needs, and her brain develops for a world that will meet her needs as long as she's willing to ask.

Responsivity is not just good for attachment and emotional security, though. As you become more efficient at communicating with each other, eventually baby will need to make very little effort to get results. Generally, a baby who is used to getting a response will learn that he doesn't need to launch into a full-throated wail every time when a mere whimper or wiggle will do. Babies' personalities differ, and some babies are more excitable than others. That's okay, too, and we'll talk about how to handle those babies a little later in this chapter.

WHY BABIES CRY

Crying is seen only in the young of animal species that are intensely social. In discussing humans, we are talking about a species that is born unable to run from predators or forage for food, and infants therefore need to solicit help from capable adults in order to survive. By using this strategy, the infant increases her chance of survival. When infants cry and the adults around them respond appropriately, the result is a harmonious cooperation that helps make the animals that use this adaptation wildly successful.

Different kinds of human cries mean different things and signal different levels of distress. Primates, a group that includes humans, generally only exhibit crying behavior when separated from their parent, a situation that, in the wild, is usually life-threatening. The human infant sound that Westerners think of as a cry—the full-throated, open-mouthed wail that can be heard meters away—is a distress signal that falls into a similar category.

It is important to understand that crying is a late cue. Babies also make whimpering noises, grunts, and subtle body language cues well before they start to cry. In the case of hunger, babies will signal for 15 minutes before they start to cry. Once they've progressed to a full cry, their nervous system is signaling that they're in life-threatening danger.

Although the baby might not be in danger, his body thinks it's dying. Consequently, his heart rate increases, blood pressure rises, and levels of stress hormones in his blood go up.

As a result of our preoccupied, multitasking, hang-on-just-a-sec way of life, Western babies spend a good deal of time each day in this high-stress state. However, leaving babies in a high-stress state hasn't always been the norm, and it is not the norm in parts of the world where babies' needs are anticipated and their signals receive an active response. During much of human history, infants did not spend much time crying throughout the day. Humans were not always at the top of the food chain, and crying attracted attention they would prefer to avoid.

Humans are not very well adapted to spending so much time in this state of acute stress. Anthropologists say that we are pushing infants to, and past, the edge of their biological constraints. The infant brain doubles in size in the first year, and the conditions under which this occurs tell the brain how to grow. A baby who is left to cry is getting a message that, "This world is not safe. It is not predictable. Be on alert and conserve your resources."

DIVING A LITTLE DEEPER ON THE CONCEPT OF RESPONSIVITY

Much of the time, especially in the early months, responsivity means responding quickly. Babies, even older ones, have a need to be responded to in a timely manner. Stress crying and self-soothing are largely cultural myths that don't have any basis in infant behavioral science.

However, as a child grows and you build your attachment, you will start to realize that responsivity means holding back sometimes, too. This is where the sensitivity skill comes in.

For example, a parent who is still working on sensitivity may wave a toy in baby's face without noticing that he's quite happy with the one he already has.

With older children, holding back may mean resisting the urge to shout, "Be careful!" when little Suzie is on the monkey bars and instead remaining steadily nearby and letting her explore.

There is mounting evidence that the hormonal feedback systems involved with breastfeeding, cuddling, and communication help increase this sort of sensitivity, or accuracy, in recognizing a child's true need. In the older childhood and teen years, this skill set becomes more complex and challenging. But with practice, time, and close attention, you will know when to leap to your child's aid and when to hang back.

Family and friends are always preferable to childcare providers due to their long-term investment in the child. But not all parents have access to familial support. Start interviewing babysitters well before you're ready to go out without baby and before you have your her, if you can. Give yourself the time to interview multiple people and collect a handful of names of some really great people so you have them ready when you need them. Join some local like-minded parenting groups as soon as possible and start building a friend group. They can be a great resource for recommendations, and some groups trade childcare nights: "You go on a date this week, I'll go next. We'll watch each other's children." Other parents are an invaluable resource.

I'm not saying that we need to recreate some kind of Pleistocene Eden in which babies are carried around in antelope-skin slings and never, ever cry, and we all ditch our smartphones and instead sit around all day staring lovingly into our babies' eyes. But through this evolutionary understanding of our babies, we can perhaps be more mindful of the fact that infancy is the closest we ever get in our lives to pure, evolved biology. Babies aren't aware that your life situation isn't safe for bed sharing, that their bottle needs to be boiled so they don't get sick, or that you've got work in the morning.

Even if you change nothing at all, I hope that gaining a little deeper understanding of why your baby is the way she is and what she's trying to say to you will be therapeutic in and of itself. If you do nothing different, I think that learning to read infant signaling language can open up a whole new world for you, making you feel more in control and confident as a parent and more connected with your child.

Here are some wonderful things your baby already knows how to say and some tips for how you can know he's saying it:

"I'm hungry." (Early hunger.) Little babies often need a feeding upon waking. The first hunger cue looks like stirring with eyes closed as they come out of sleep. Baby will open his mouth and stick out his tongue. He'll begin lip licking and smacking, rooting, turning his head side to side, looking for a breast. (It's a reflex, so bottle-fed babies will do it, too.) Baby may bring his hand to his mouth. Rooting and bringing the hand to the mouth are the two most easy-to-spot hunger cues, so now that you know them, you may start seeing them in every baby on the street. Have you ever tickled a baby's cheek with your finger? He will move his mouth toward it and try to get your finger in his mouth.

"I'm really hungry. Feed me now!" (Mid-hunger.) The stirring progresses to something more like squirming or fidgeting. Movements become slightly more vigorous, frequent, and agitated. A baby who is being held upright against your chest will dive for a nipple, regardless of who is holding her. She'll try to suck on anything within reach—her hand, her arm, a toy, the nursing pillow, your shirt, your face. This is an intense hunger cue that means crying is coming soon. Breathing will become more rapid. Baby will start to vocalize, using noises best described as fussing. She may start to cry a little.

"Everything I've tried hasn't worked, and now I'm scared and uncomfortable. Calm me first, then meet my need." (Late hunger/pain/fear.) A very hungry baby has progressed to full-on crying that you might describe as hysterical, with an open mouth, very tense body, and skin that becomes flushed red. Baby's body is very tense, hands are balled up into tight fists, and movements are out of control and uncoordinated. At this level of agitation, the need is dual: the need that started the whole thing and, now that baby

is all worked up, a need for calming. If the original need was hunger, his head may be moving from side to side in an intense rooting reflex.

"I'm full. Please pull the breast/bottle away." During a feed, you will see baby's hand slowly open from a clenched fist to a relaxed and open hand. She will stop sucking and let go of the bottle. She may push the bottle away with her hands. If you put the bottle back in baby's mouth after she pushes it away, she may suck a little, but that doesn't mean she's hungry. Sucking is a reflex, so a full baby will take a few sucks, stop, and swallow to prevent choking. A hungry baby sucks vigorously.

"I'm ready to learn—play with me!" Baby's body is calm and relaxed, and his arm and leg movements are more coordinated, not flailing. His eyes are bright and looking around, especially at you. This calm, alert state is optimal for learning. It's a great time to talk or sing to your baby and play games. It is also a good time to introduce baby to a new situation, such as trying out a sling for the first time. For newborns, this state doesn't usually last very long, sometimes just a couple of minutes, so keep an eye out for increasingly agitated movements that may indicate increasing hunger or overstimulation.

"I am getting sleepy." Baby needs you to help him fall asleep. This one can seem similar to the quiet alert state, except this baby's eyes are not bright. This baby is not looking so much as staring. He may start to yawn. A baby who isn't swaddled may start to rub his ears or eyes.

"I am overstimulated." This is a common message that is often overlooked in our desire to interact with baby. Babies are easily overwhelmed and tire easily. Sometimes, if you get too close to a baby or if the activity is too loud or has gone on too long, she will start to turn away. This is an attempt to disengage. Some babies may also arch their whole body

away or bring their hands up to their face or push things away. If the message is not received and the activity goes on, they'll start to fuss. This cue often coincides with tiredness but can also be brought on by discomfort, such as a wet diaper. In the absence of something obvious, such as an older sibling playing a little-too-intense game of peek-a-boo, this cue is a signal to examine different things in the baby's environment to see what the problem might be. You can stop the activity, try turning the lights down, turn on some white noise, or even disrobe her and wrap her in a blanket to reduce her physical stimulation.

"I know you're here, and I am trying to calm down, but it's hard." This one isn't really covered in parenting classes, but I like to point it out because this sign is an encouraging one for parents to notice. It often appears while a baby is crying, especially older babies and toddlers. It sounds like a hiccup or a few short breaths taken while crying. This is a sign that the child is attempting to control her breath and calm down, and it's also a sign of emotional regulation skills. Sometimes, when baby is crying uncontrollably and there isn't much to be done about it (such as in the car or during a medical procedure), it may be helpful to you to simply notice your child's attempts to settle, provide some soft touch and verbal reassurance, and be encouraged that she is learning good coping skills—from you!

WHEN IN DOUBT, WHIP IT OUT

You may find that life is a bit easier if you respond to most fussing with feeding first. Just like adults, babies' ability to handle life's problems is positively correlated with the fullness of their stomachs. So, when baby is waking up from a nap and starting to fuss and you're not sure if it's diaper or food related, your odds are likely better if you fill baby's tummy with half an ounce or half a breast, wait for her to calm down, then change her.

THE IMPORTANCE OF SOOTHING BABIES

Just as adult and older child temperaments differ, babies differ in their level of excitability. Some babies are set off more easily for longer periods and have more difficulty settling. In a 2016 study, anthropologist James McKenna and his colleagues offer a theory that some babies, around age three to four months, get stuck in a crying loop, in which they lose control of their breath and cannot stop crying, which in turn causes them to become afraid. For these babies, it is important to rule out medical causes for the crying with the help of your pediatrician and other relevant specialists.

Remember, helping a baby to co-regulate by holding them while crying will help them to mirror the calming impact of your comfort. Like us, children want to be comforted when they cry, so holding children while they cry is, in fact, doing something. Allow this knowledge to empower you and give you peace in the chaos. You are everything to your child, even when his world is falling apart. Inconsolable crying is common in younger babies during the evenings and is often related to overstimulation. These babies will cluster feed and seemingly refuse to be happy from before dinner until bedtime. For these babies, it helps to turn down the lights or the TV, reduce any sort of intense sensory input, and provide their favorite soothing techniques, such as movement, swaddling, and white noise. Even if baby continues to cry, try the technique for at least five minutes before giving up and switching to another method. On average, crying frequency hits a peak between three and four months, then starts to fall off after that.

RESPONDING TO SENSITIVE BABIES

Babies with excitable temperaments sometimes grow out of their excitability, and sometimes they grow up to be excitable children and, later, excitable teenagers. Other kids are super chill as babies, but then when a new sibling arrives, they suddenly become drama kings or queens.

Renowned early childhood educator Mary Sheedy Kurcinka and Dr. Sears both talk about a revolutionary way of thinking about children with excitable temperaments. First, they suggest that we change our language. Instead of calling her a "difficult" child, call her "spirited" or "high needs." This change in language reflects the fact that whatever is bothering the child, be it an undiagnosed condition or merely an extremely excitable temperament, it is unintentional on the part of the child and not a result of poor parenting. Then, the experts recommend that we meet the child's needs. Research on spirited children suggests that they are highly reactive to parenting style (in this context, sometimes also called "orchid" children, since orchids grow to tremendous beauty under very specific conditions). When children are parented with sensitivity, outcomes are positive in the extreme. These children grow up to be innovators, leaders, and passionate artists—movers and shakers. In other words, you get out of your children what you put into them. The challenging part is that parenting can be a real energy sucker. Whereas other kids need buckets full of love, reassurance, and attention, these kiddos need wheelbarrows full—and sometimes, it seems, dump trucks full. But take heart, exhausted parent, because all this energy you're expending is worth it. Science says so.

IF YOU'RE A SINGLE PARENT

Believe it or not, there are both pros and cons to being a single parent. For example, parenting responsively is easier in some ways for single parents because they don't have another opinion to contend with, their attention isn't divided, and they have more room in the bed for cuddling. On the other hand, not having a partner is also much harder for obvious reasons, such as the fact that you can't take a break because there's nobody to hand baby off to.

If you are working, cosleeping is a great tool for making up for the time you can't spend with your child during the day. Also, babywearing is like having an extra set of hands and makes it more convenient to do things, including respond to your child. Babywearing helps when you are a working parent because it gives the child more cuddle time that he may not be getting in daycare.

IF YOUR CHILD IS HOSPITALIZED

Hospital stays take an emotional toll on everyone because of the health concerns and the discomfort produced by all the interaction required by strangers—sometimes painful interaction. And of course, stress can be contagious. Enter the tears. Inconsolable crying is one of the most heart-wrenching components of hospital procedures and illness.

To complicate matters, even the most skilled hospital staff may not be particularly accommodating to your desire to respond to and minimize your child's crying. Hospital workers deal with crying children and adults all day long, so many of them acclimate to the sound of crying and may not take it seriously, which could be a coping mechanism that they're not aware of. Hospital workers may be the health experts, but you are your baby's expert and her advocate. You'll want to monitor who interacts with your child and how, and your job is to speak up for your child. Do not be afraid to ask questions like these:

- What are the risks and benefits of this procedure?
- What happens if we do not do this procedure?
- What are the alternatives to this procedure?
- Can we have some time to prepare my child first?
- Does this procedure absolutely need to be done this way?
- Can I hold my child during the procedure?
- What is your plan for pain management during and after the procedure?

HOW TO HELP YOUR HOSPITAL VISIT GO SMOOTHLY

Talk about it. If the hospital visit is planned and if the child is old enough, try to prepare him on some level for what is going to happen. Many parents avoid talking about the hospital for fear of scaring the child, but that can sometimes backfire. A child who has a chance to mentally prepare can call up coping mechanisms and more readily begin the mental recovery process. You can prepare the child in an age-appropriate way, without giving him any more detail than he needs, and reassure him that you will be there with him and that he can do this.

Ask for intervention staff. Find out if your hospital has a child life specialist. This is a mental health professional whose job is to use specialized, play-based techniques to help children cope with hospital environments and procedures.

Another specialist you might consider asking for is a pain nurse. Pain is a psychologically and socially complex phenomenon, particularly for children and infants, who cannot necessarily communicate their experience. A pain nurse can help tailor the pain relief given to your child and stay on top of the pain, addressing it before it gets worse.

Offer liquid comfort. For infants and very young children, you might consider using sugar water for shots, blood draws, and other brief but painful procedures. Sugar water, given in very tiny amounts, has been shown to have a pain-relieving effect on infants during vaccination procedures. Hospitals may have glucose drops on hand, as they are often used in neonatal intensive care units, or you can mix your own by stirring one packet of sugar (about a teaspoon) into 10 mL (two teaspoons) of water and giving baby a sip about a minute or two before the procedure. This is a rare and special situation—typically, babies under six months old should not be given sugar or water that isn't already in their regular food, except for medical reasons. For breastfed babies, it helps to breastfeed immediately prior to and after the procedure for comfort. If you are bottle feeding, you can bottle feed in the same way you do at home—anything you think might help.

Cuddle in. Whenever possible, cuddles both during and after the procedure will make your little one feel less alone and help minimize the trauma. Studies on crying babies found that babies who are held while they cry had a diminished cortisol response compared to babies who were left alone to cry. This means that even if you cannot stop your baby from crying, holding her and talking to her in a soothing voice helps her, even if you can't tell on the outside.

FINDING RESPONSIVE CAREGIVERS

If you cannot be with your child, take care to find caregivers who are sensitive to your child's needs. Family members are great, even when they don't do everything the way you want them to, because they are invested in your child for the long term. When choosing a childcare setting for an infant or very young child, you can't go wrong erring on the side of sensitivity and choosing a high caregiver to child ratio over academic rigor. Ask about turnover rates if applicable and talk to the caregivers and try to get to know them as people. For a great guide to finding care geared toward attachment-minded parents, check out psychologist Tracy Cassels' *Finding Daycare* (see Resources, page 117).

WHEN SLEEP TRAINING FEELS LIKE THE ONLY OPTION

Recognize that your tiredness is determined by not just the amount of sleep you get but also the quality of your sleep. Things that can affect sleep quality, as well as quantity, include caffeine, anxiety, watching movies too late at night, and eating too close to bedtime. Practice sleep hygiene. Implement environmental changes, like dimming the lights and switching off screens, which can signal to the body that it is time to prepare for sleep. Light is important because blue-spectrum light, like the kind that comes from screens, can suppress the production of melatonin for up to an hour after exposure.

By practicing sleep hygiene, breastfeeding families are giving their babies a natural dose of melatonin, just as nature intended. Since the concentration of melatonin and other circadian rhythm-regulating factors in human milk vary throughout the day, science suggests that labeling expressed breast milk with the time of day and trying to match feedings to time of pumping may help babies develop a more regular sleep pattern. Giving the baby a warm bath right after dinner signals to her body that it is time to start winding down.

Sometimes, the thing to do is just ride it out. Attachment parents may be afraid to share their frustrations about their child's behavior because they're afraid that their friends will respond with pressure to abandon the path they have chosen. Attachment parents may feel touched out and perhaps even resentful after three days in a row of their sick two-year-old marathon nursing like a newborn. Or parents may be so tired from breastsleeping their high-needs baby that they walked out to the car without their keys—or their pants. Well-meaning, childless friends, or perhaps other parents with somewhat different values, may, out of compassion, feel that it is their job to grant the parent permission to wean that kid already, put her in her own room, or encourage the parent to put his foot down. The only person you need permission from, to do anything, is yourself. Changing your mind on any one of the Baby B's is always a choice. However, many parents, I find, just want to vent. Parents just want someone to hold space for them.

Find that friend—the non-judgy one. If your friend is not the particularly perceptive type, you may have to flat-out say, "Hey, can I vent at you for a minute? I just need someone to listen and not try to fix my problems." And keep those lines of communication open with your partner or co-parent.

But also, find ways to cope. Maybe that load of laundry can wait. Maybe there's a friend that you know would jump up and help if you asked, who can sit and watch cartoons with the kids for a couple of hours while you catch up on sleep. This is the season of your life where you call in those favors. Because one day, you'll be past all this, but you'll still remember it, and you will happen upon a younger friend or family member who is now in the throes of it themselves. And at that time, you will pay it forward because that is what Villagers do.

WHEN CIRCUMSTANCES DON'T PROVIDE US WITH A CHOICE

What if you work 80 hours a week and you feel like your life will fall apart if you have to spend 40 minutes rocking your baby to sleep every night? There is hope on the horizon! A multinational group of scientists is developing a new sleep program to replace the old sleep-training approach. This program is the only sleep solution developed by scientists with a history of research in the field of human infant sleep, and it is being field-tested as we speak. This solution could be a game changer for parents who prefer not to let their babies cry. Scientists call it the Possums Sleep Intervention because the program was partially developed in Australia, and *little possum* is a term of endearment that Australians use for their babies. The name might also have something to do with the fact that possums are nocturnal.

Unlike many of the self-professed coaching or consulting peddlers out there, the Possums program doesn't require crying and is based on cross-disciplinary science. The program integrates evolutionary science and neuroscience, and the methodology focuses on practicing good sleep hygiene and understanding the nuances of infant sleep. The goals are holistic—to improve not just sleep quantity but also quality and to alleviate parental stress, all without pathologizing normal infant behavior and potentially compromising breastfeeding. And the program has had promising results. Parents who participated in the program reported less stress, less concern about sleep problems such as night waking and daytime naps, and better quality of life. See the Resources section (page 118) for more information about the Possums program.

Since the Sears books were published, baby trainers have stepped up their marketing game. They're aware that baby training gets a bad rap and that it is increasingly discouraged by medical professionals. (Most authorities at least consider baby training unsafe to implement before the baby is six months.) These days, baby trainers often soften their image by referring to themselves as coaches or consultants. The vast majority of sleep interventionists operate in a sort of bait-and-switch manner. They do not make it very obvious on their websites or social media accounts, but if you examine their marketing more closely, or if you're lucky enough to get a peek at one of their personalized intervention plans that they give to their clients, you start to notice that they're usually peddling pseudoscientific myths in order to sell their services.

The reason for the bait-and-switch approach is obvious. Approaches to infant sleep solutions that acknowledge that night waking is normal and not pathological aren't marketable in our culture. Our culture is one that expects a certain level of convenience from babies. And, at the end of the day, if sleep professionals do not deliver the results a client expects (or the results that the family's circumstances demand), they aren't going to get paid.

There are a few—very few—sleep professionals that seem to be making their business work while also retaining their scientific integrity. Tracy Cassels, owner of EvolutionaryParenting.com, holds a PhD in psychology and consults over the phone and through video conference from her home in Ontario, Canada. Lyndsey Hookway is an IBCLC based in the UK and is the developer of a sleep consultant training program called Holistic Sleep Coaching. Lyndsey's program was designed to address the problem of sleep professionals peddling pseudoscientific myths and methodologies, and it is the only accredited sleep coach training program that I have seen. I've included materials by these two trailblazing professionals in the Resources section on page 117. Neither one of these individuals solicited my endorsement. I just love that they offer ethical, science-based solutions in a world where they could be making a great deal more money if they strayed from the science. But they have stayed the course and weathered the consequences.

Even with all the best resources, every parent experiences a moment, at some point in their parenting journey, where they feel like they might completely lose it if they have to spend one more minute listening to baby cry. If you ever feel like you might hurt your baby or things just become utterly unbearable, it's okay to put baby down, in a safe place, walk into another room for a few minutes, breathe, and then come back. No baby ever died of crying, but sadly the same can't be said for those that are shaken in a moment of parental frustration or overwhelm. In most cases, though, your baby is perfect just the way she is. Understand that it is not your baby but our Village that needs to change. In Chapter 6, I will talk about the reasons parents find themselves overwhelmed.

But for now, remember the fleeting nature of this season of your life: This time won't last forever.

HOW DOES SLEEP TRAINING IMPACT ATTACHMENT AND DEVELOPMENT?

I know attachment parents who did some version of cry-it-out. So far, no one has showed up at their door and revoked their Attachment Parenting International membership card. More common, though, is parents who desperately want to sleep train, but simply never get around to it because they know they won't be able to emotionally bear the sound of their child crying for hours every night for several nights in a row. Some parents try to sleep train but can't make it through the process. (Being unable to listen to your baby cry is not a sign of weakness, by the way. Last I heard, compassion for a crying person is a desirable personality trait.) Usually, those parents you know who seem to have glided blissfully through their early years of nighttime parenting probably made it through that time by a combination of luck and accident.

If you sleep trained because of misinformation or because, due to your circumstances, you felt you had no choice, you can heal from the experience and move on. This is one of many things in parenting that didn't pan out the way you planned. You can't change the past. You can take the new information you've learned and implement it in the future if you so choose.

Parents who have let their babies cry it out inevitably wonder if they have done lasting harm to their child, but as far as I understand there isn't conclusive research on the topic. Ascertaining the long-term effects of sleep training would be difficult because there are a lot of ethical barriers to designing a scientific study that would answer that question with a high degree of certainty. Instead, let's focus on how you can move forward from this.

To begin with, focus on your child. Dr. Tracy Cassels advises that parents continue parenting responsively, as you have already probably been doing, judging by your reading choice today. But Dr. Cassels suggests you can be particularly sensitive to your child around bedtime and through the night. Try to notice subtle changes in your child's behavior or demeanor around bedtime and respond in a compassionate and gentle manner. Validate your child's feelings, even in babyhood. Hold space while your little one works though these feelings and have faith that you deserve your child's trust.

Then, focus on yourself. First, understand that we live in a society that is rare among nations in its unfriendliness to normal infant sleep physiology. Understand that the phenomenon of sleep training, in a larger sense, is a cycle of culturally perpetuated abuse. By forcing parents to return to work sooner than they're ready to, by isolating nuclear families from their historical Village, and by depriving parents of sleep, we are effectively torturing young parents. (Sleep deprivation is actually on the Geneva Convention's list of prohibited interrogation techniques.) In turn, many parents are often left with no choice or no coping mechanisms, and the abuse, whether intentional or not, is perpetuated onto the next generation. Try and reframe the narrative: Perhaps sleep training wasn't something you did so much as something that happened to your family.

After you have recognized the larger forces that were at play in your circumstances, examine the ways in which you actively resisted those forces and focus on the things you did well when it came to nighttime parenting. Before you did the sleep training, how long did you resist doing it? What strategies did you use to cope with your child's night-waking behavior? How did you show up for your baby at night? How did you show up during the day? Examine the sleep training process itself and your feelings toward it. Chances are, you at least found it stressful. Acknowledge that the unpleasantness you felt is a good thing; it means that you are a good person who has compassion for your child. What, if anything, did you do during the process to make it easier on your child? Did you do a lot of research to find the gentlest method you could? Did you decide to do sleep training as quickly as possible, like ripping off a bandage, to spare your child prolonged suffering? If you stopped the process before its planned conclusion, try to reframe this not as weakness or a failed attempt but as a reflection of your personal boundaries. Whether out of exhaustion or compassion, you did not adhere to dogma at all costs, and this is a sign that you are a reasonable human being.

And grant yourself the gift of forgiveness, because one thing is for sure: The person whose opinion matters most already has forgiven you.

Also, remember that returning to cosleeping is always an option. You can move your baby's crib back into your room or offer a toddler bed as an option. This is not a step backward—it is righting a wrong. In most cases, people are not willing to jeopardize the sleep time that they've secured through the difficult process of sleep training. In that case, pursue the other Baby B's. Use bottlenursing and babywearing to stuff your day full of closeness and contact and validation. Please don't feel like these practices are going to spoil the baby or ruin your sleep training. It is normal and important for babies to need contact and reassurance and flexibility.

Look for ways to connect with your child during the day. Focus on floor time, which is a dedicated block of time where you turn off the phone and put it in another room and focus just on your child for a 20-minute block of time every day. Let your child lead the play and allow yourself to become completely immersed in your child's world. There is strong evidence that floor time makes a tangible difference in the lives of parents who work away from home, travel, or otherwise cannot be with their child for huge blocks of time. There is no reason to think that floor time can't work for children who sleep separately as well.

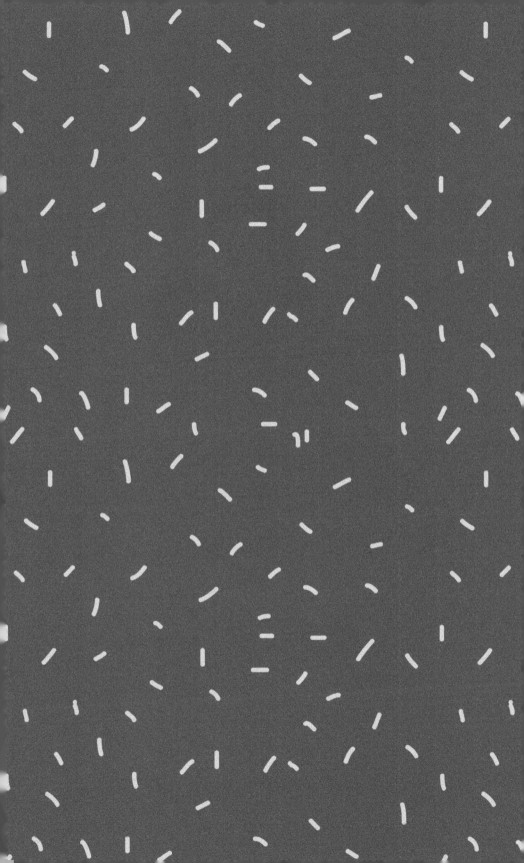

CHAPTER SIX

BALANCE, BOUNDARIES, AND BEYOND

YOU'RE PARENT ENOUGH, THE VILLAGE JUST ISN'T VILLAGE ENOUGH

It's important to have a balanced view of yourself as a parent. For many modern parents, with all the talk of optimizing child outcomes, guilt over not being enough is a constant companion that has overstayed its welcome.

More and more, people acknowledge that mothering needs to be counted among the occupations that are experiencing high rates of burnout. The popular solution, self-care, isn't enough.

In the US, a very individualist culture, failure has been internalized by parents and moms in particular. People, families, and mothers are living and operating in silos. Once members of the so-called Village, people have now hunkered down in their own silos, each trying to raise the family alone.

The history of human parenting tells a very different story. Most anthropologists agree that humans evolved under social conditions that were pretty egalitarian by today's standards. We raised very resource-expensive babies with rapidly growing brains with only the help of a group. For example, until relatively recently in the scope of human history, an exhausted or sick new mother would have had help nursing her baby from sisters, aunts, and even her own mother, allowing her to get some rest. And since breastfeeding was normalized in all cultures prior to 100 or so years ago, there was very little risk of skipping a feed and compromising a mother's milk supply like there is now. All new mothers knew the importance of putting the baby to the breast on demand and extracting milk often.

Breastfeeding mothers were not ostracized, shamed, or told to hide away or feed in a bathroom. Babies were welcome in public spaces. There was no marketing of products that separate babies from their parents and compromise milk supply.

Of course, I don't want to idealize the past and ignore the fact that many of these women who used to help other women are no longer available as they are pursuing fulfilling careers. But as someone who has spent a lot of time with this issue, I realize that women weren't liberated all the way. Women bear the brunt of the physiological burden of propagating our species. To that end, true liberation would be better served if birthing, breastfeeding, bottlenursing, and soothing babies was treated in a way that reflects how objectively valuable these processes are to society as a whole.

When parents are doing the best they can but still feeling less-than, they often hurry to cast blame on themselves when perhaps society should take the blame. Your Village failed to show up for you. The Village is failing Western families the world over. The Village has forgotten how babies work. It has, in many ways, forgotten what it is. Both the cause (parents putting too much pressure on themselves) and the proposed solution (self-care) are individualist, but the problem is social and structural. How is this supposed to help you now? Parents are the last people who have time and energy to engage in a social change movement.

I'm not going to lie, it's hard. I hope, though, that simply understanding society's role in making your job as a parent counterintuitive is therapeutic and allows you to let go of at least some of your guilt. Understand that you are attempting to parent sensitively and responsively in a world that is actively working to sell you strollers and cribs and devices that separate you from your baby, cast doubt on your milk supply, divide you from other parents, and deny you rights—all with a general goal of profit. So, in choosing to use attachment parenting—in whatever way works for your family—please be kind to yourself and celebrate every little victory. Every accomplishment, no matter how small, is a tiny act of rebellion on behalf of your baby and against the status quo.

I hope that understanding that humans have always worked together in raising humans frees you to accept help from the loyal villagers you may be lucky enough to count on and to actively ask for help when you need it. Someday, your kids will be grown, and it will be your turn to help a new parent out.

GETTING OVER THE NEW PARENT OVERWHELM

Use the tools you have to just go about the business of living your life. Maybe not the life you had before, but one that is engaged in the community.

Take your baby out and about. It might feel overwhelming to think about, but staying home and being isolated contributes the most to that oppressive dread and hopelessness. This is where babywearing really shines. Wear baby to the store, or to a cafe, and strike up a conversation with the barista. Will your baby cry? Probably, yeah. Just deal with it and don't apologize. Leave the nursing cover at home, and ignore anyone who gives you dirty looks. You don't have time for that.

When your baby cries at restaurants, or your toddler throws a tantrum, don't underestimate the magic of getting up and just taking them outside for a minute. You're not doing this to spare the people around you, because screw them. There's something magical about the open air that just kind of hits a kid's reset button. Walk and bounce the baby in a carrier. With a toddler, hold them and walk back and forth while they work through their little moment, or hold their hand and walk. Ride it out, then come back to the table.

An easy trick is to take your baby to the park. Yes, I said take your itty bitty baby to the park. It's a great thing to do between 3 and 6 months old. Instead of laying your baby down inside for tummy time, grab a blanket—and maybe a book (for you!)—and find a playground with lots of preschoolers and kindergarteners. Find a bench and just lay your baby down on a blanket in front of you, and let them watch and listen to the laughing children while you read or let your mind wander a bit. I guarantee, at some point, one of the other kids will wander over and your baby will have a fabulous time looking at her new friend.

MATERNAL HEALTH MATTERS

In our culture, we tend to overtreat and undertreat pregnant women. Pregnancy is not a sickness, but in US hospitals pregnancy is treated as such, and things snowball from there. Health-care providers look for things that are wrong that aren't there and many unnecessary interventions can be more harmful than helpful. In overtreating, physicians can miss things that are wrong.

When I was hospitalized with HELLP syndrome at 37 weeks, I remember being treated as if I didn't want to be pregnant anymore. I was dying. Ultimately, I think that I almost died for the same reason they overtreat women who come into the hospital looking for a low-intervention birth: Health-care professionals often don't listen to the mother.

I lost all rights to my body while I was in the hospital. I could see that my blood pressure was stroke-level, yet nobody in the room was talking about me. I felt alone, scared, and insignificant. I got the impression that the baby I was gestating was more important to this world than I was. I felt like a host. I felt like I was suddenly worthless. I remember feeling so much shame and guilt. I cared more about my baby than my own life, but I felt awful for caring about my own life at all.

Our values are reflected in our maternal mortality ratios in this country, which are the worst of all the wealthy countries (despite how much money we throw at the problem). The numbers are even worse for women of color, which in some parts of the country have mortality rates as high as what is seen in developing countries. And according to one of my favorite medical researchers, obstetrician Neel Shah, this is largely because hospital staff often do not listen to mothers when they try to tell them something is wrong.

In an article by Marcia Frellick, Alison Stuebe, another rock star obstetrician, put it bluntly: "In our current system of care, the baby is the candy and the mother is the wrapper. Once the candy is out of the wrapper, the wrapper is cast aside."

When you're pregnant or in labor it's not just okay to prioritize and advocate for your own health—it's important.

You've Got This

Even if you do nothing differently after reading this book, I hope that knowing a bit more about why babies are the way they are and that you are not alone is therapeutic for you. I hope you see that attachment parenting is not the dogmatic parenting cult the media makes it out to be. In fact, attachment parenting is fundamentally anti-dogmatic because it invites you to parent not according to cultural trends but according to your long-evolved instincts, with modifications according to your family circumstances, and of course, informed by science. Attachment parenting is having faith in your natural urges and tendencies as a loving parent—what could be more human than that?

Always try to remember that sensitive parenting means being sensitive to your and your child's needs. As you allow yourself to be the parent you choose to be, your confidence will grow along with your child. High five! Every little drop of breast milk, every cuddle, every midnight shuffle to the crib, every song, every caress is a tiny triumph for your baby over a culture that wants you to replace those things with a plastic toy, a pacifier, or a noise machine. It's your turn to parent. Trust your gut and savor the beautiful journey on the path that *you* have chosen.

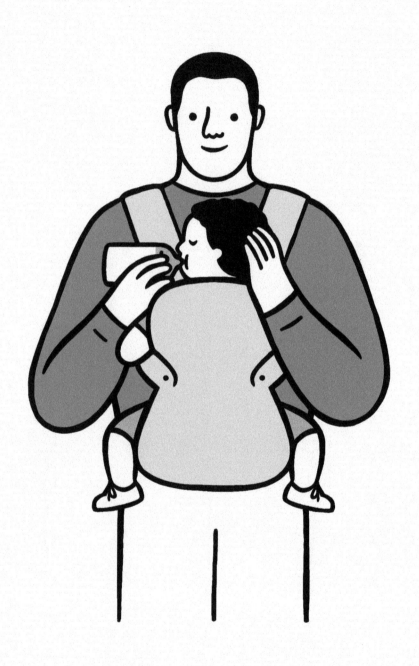

Glossary

Adaptation - A behavior, physical feature, or biological process that accidentally emerges in a species over the course of evolution, and turns out to be useful for helping that species survive and thrive.

Ainsworth, Mary - A student of John Bowlby, Mary Ainsworth developed a method of testing attachment in the laboratory, using a simple test called the "Strange Situation" test. Since this test was developed in the 1970s and longitudinal studies have been performed, this test has been consistently shown to predict long-term outcomes such as empathy, emotional security, language skills, and relationship quality in adulthood.

Alloparenting/Allocare - Coined by biologist Edward O. Wilson, "alloparenting" it is a term that scientists use to refer to any situation where an infant or juvenile animal is fed or cared for by someone other than its parent. It is a fascinating phenomenon found mostly only in highly social species and is believed to be a key part of the story of how humans became so intelligent. Allocare is a less-popular variant whose definition is still fluid, sometimes used in reference specifically to the Western phenomenons of daycare, nannying, and babysitting.

Attachment - The quality of relationship that a child has with their primary caregiver that loosely translates to trust and a feeling of being protected and safe. A child is said to be "securely" attached when he or she exhibits a normal response to psychological tests designed to measure the quality of his or her attachment to their primary caregiver. In Western culture, we tend to judge early "independence" as a sign of healthy development; however, a healthy infant will become distressed when separated from their parent, and calm down relatively quickly when the parent returns. Security in the context of attachment is a slightly different thing than the colloquial use of the term "security."
(See: Security [emotional].)

Attachment parenting - Developed in the 1980s and '90s by pediatrician Bill Sears and his wife, nurse Martha Sears, attachment parenting is a set of science-based tools for raising a more compassionate, resilient child. It is not the same thing as Attachment Theory, but it is based on its principles.

Attachment Theory - An area of psychological research that focuses on emotional security and human relationships. It was developed by influential psychologist John Bowlby beginning in the 1960s based on cross-cultural observations. The theory was then tested in the lab by his student, Mary Ainsworth.

Bonding - A colloquial term referring to the feeling of closeness or shared emotion that unites two people. It is different from "attachment" in that it is a loosely defined concept that does not have a corresponding test.

Bottlenursing - A method for bottle feeding a baby, in development by Bridget McGann, that carefully studies what science has illuminated about the behavioral components of breastfeeding, and adapts them for bottle feeding families, with the goal of fostering healthy social and emotional development. Major components of bottlenursing include what is known among lactation consultants as either "paced feeding" or "responsive bottle feeding." See Chapter 3 for the rundown on how to bottlenurse.

Bowlby, John - An influential British psychologist who is famous for developing Attachment Theory beginning in the 1960s based on cross-cultural observations.

Breastsleeping - A portmanteau of "breastfeeding" and "sleeping" developed by anthropologist James McKenna in his 2015 article in *Acta Paediatrica* "There is no such thing as infant sleep, there is no such thing as breastfeeding, there is only breastsleeping" to address the problem of research and public discourse surrounding breastfeeding separately from infant sleep and infant sleep separately from breastfeeding. Breastfeeding and same-surface cosleeping evolved alongside each other and are, therefore, inextricably linked. McKenna coined this term to encourage researchers and parents alike to understand that neither can be fully understood without also considering the other, as well as to emphasize the fact that breastsleeping is fundamentally different physiologically than bed sharing outside of the context of exclusive breastfeeding (and that the latter, therefore, is not recommended).

Co-regulation - A way for babies to calm their nervous systems by mirroring the regulated responses of their adult caregivers.

Cortisol - A steroid hormone that, in small amounts over short periods of time, plays an important role in motivation and alertness. In parents, it helps motivate them to respond to their baby's cries or other sounds. In too-high levels for prolonged periods of time, however, cortisol can negatively affect both parental health and infant health. In the parent, too much cortisol can contribute to mood disorders and memory loss. Less is known how too much cortisol might affect infant development, but it is known that, as part of the sympathetic nervous system response, cortisol stops digestion, and can affect the infant's ability to absorb nutrients and grow. Cortisol is also present in breast milk, and scientists are still studying the role that it plays in the development of the nursling, but they advise that fears about cortisol in the breastmilk of a stressed mother is not an advisable reason to cease breastfeeding. The benefits of breastfeeding still outweigh any risk that may be associated with cortisol in breast milk.

Cue - Body language or verbalization that babies use to indicate a need. See Chapter 5 for more about how babies communicate.

Ecological niche - The "ideal environment" for a given species. In other words, it is the environment and conditions that shaped a given species' physiology and behavior, and is therefore the environment in which that species thrives best. If an animal or organism is put into an environment that is too different from their ecological niche, they may become sick or develop unhealthy behavior.

Evolution - A fundamental process of biology by which species changed over very long periods of time. The main force behind this process is natural selection, which shapes the physiology and behavior of a species through eliminating traits and behaviors that do not work well in a particular environment, and passing on traits and behaviors that do work well (that are "adaptive") and help the species thrive. Things like birth, breastfeeding, breast-sleeping, and infant behavior are highly consequential processes that underwent intense "selective pressure" at various points in our evolutionary history, where the stakes are high and various features either made our broke our success as a species. Many of these behaviors still persist today, and attachment parenting tries to work with these behaviors rather than against them.

Kangaroo care (a.k.a. "skin-to-skin") - The practice of holding baby against your chest with both the parent and the baby minimally clothed in a way that allows for full skin-to-skin contact on the front of both the baby and the holder's bodies. This practice has been shown to help regulate baby's temperature, heart rate, and breathing, and fosters stress relief and healthy absorption of nutrients (and therefore growth). Most of the research in this area has been done on premature babies, but increasingly medical practitioners are recognizing that there is no reason to assume that this practice won't benefit term babies as well, and many parents are being offered an opportunity to do kangaroo care immediately following birth. Attachment parenting invites parents to continue this practice at home, and throughout the first year of baby's life, to support healthy physical and emotional regulation, as well as to maximize the efficiency of baby's calorie use, thereby decreasing the need for supplementation with donated milk or formula. Kangaroo care is discussed at length in Chapter 2.

Micro-niche - This term refers to the parent's body, which is the micro-environment, or micro-niche, that human infants are adapted to. Every species has an "ecological niche"—an ideal environment that shaped their physiology and helps them thrive. Human infants evolved under conditions where they were always being held and breastfed, which was very important in those times because humans were not the top of the food chain back then, and any amount of crying would attract predators. Adult humans are very adaptable and can thrive in a remarkably huge variety of environments; their infants, however, are happiest when they are being held—particularly skin-to-skin. This makes the parent's body, coupled with breastfeeding, a sort of ecological niche unto its own, nested within the parent's larger environment—"a niche within a niche." In our discussions of kangaroo care and bottlenursing in Chapter 2, we use this concept as a way to try and help mimic the conditions that breastfeeding helps to create, to try and help baby feel safe and secure, and foster healthy growth and development.

Oxytocin - A complex hormone that, like cortisol, does some "good" things and some "bad" things. Most famously, it is the cause of the milk ejection reflex (a.k.a. "letdown"), uterine contractions, orgasm, and feelings of closeness and bonding between people of different relations (and even our pets!). Less famously, oxytocin can be a culprit behind feelings of jealousy and outgroup paranoia. Mothers receive a little "hit" of oxytocin every time they breastfeed. This helps to reinforce the caregiving behavior, but also helps them relax and heal in the months and year following birth. In babies, the oxytocin they receive from breastmilk, as well as the oxytocin triggered in their brains from cuddling and caressing, triggers the parasympathetic nervous system, which is the process that lowers the heart rate and resumes digestion after a stressful event. In our discussion of bonding and kangaroo care in Chapter 2, in our discussion of bottlenursing in Chapter 3, and in our discussion of babywearing in Chapter 4, we attempt to help all families find ways to foster healthy levels of oxytocin in their child, to the best of their ability.

Paced feeding (a.k.a. "responsive feeding" or "baby-led bottle feeding") - A method of bottle feeding that differs dramatically from the way bottle feeding is conventionally taught and depicted on TV. It was developed to help preserve baby's breastfeeding skills when a breastfed baby must be bottle-fed, but most infant feeding specialists now recommend it be used with all babies because it helps to prevent over-feeding. In paced feeding, the carer holds the baby sitting up instead of lying down, and holds the bottle level to the ground instead of tilting it back, so that the baby has to work to draw the milk out of the nipple. The baby is allowed to take "breaks" during the feed, and the feed is ended when the baby stops actively sucking, rather than when the bottle is empty. We adapt this method to include other components in the Chapter 3 section on bottlenursing.

Responsivity - A parental skill that is focused on meeting a baby's needs, or responding, in a timely manner. For infants, this usually means responding quickly, so that the infant learns that communicating her needs is an effective strategy, and helps her expend less energy on hysterical crying. Sometimes we may be good at being sensitive (accurate) in responding to baby's needs, but not necessarily able to be responsive (quick) in that moment.

Sears, Martha - A nurse and La Leche League leader who co-developed attachment parenting with her husband William in the 1980s and '90s. She and William are parents to eight now-grown children.

Sears, William - A pediatrician who co-developed attachment parenting with his wife Martha in the 1980s and '90s. He and Martha are parents to eight now-grown children.

Security (attachment) - See: Attachment.

Security (emotional) - A child who generally perceives themselves to be safe and has well-developing emotional regulation skills can be said to be emotionally secure. Emotional security is different from attachment security but related to it in that it can be influenced by the security of attachment. (See: Attachment.)

Sensitivity - A parental skill that is focused on accurately identifying baby's needs. This accuracy in responding teaches baby to improve their own accuracy in communicating their needs. Sometimes we may be good at being responsive (quick) in meeting baby's needs in the moment, but we might need to work on being more sensitive, or accurately identifying baby's need. This gets better with practice!

Resources

Books

The Attachment Parenting Book by Dr. William Sears and Martha Sears

The Baby Book by Dr. William Sears and Martha Sears

The Breastfeeding Book (Updated ed. 2018) by Dr. William Sears and Martha Sears

Dr. Jack Newman's Guide to Breastfeeding: Updated Edition by Dr. Jack Newman and Teresa Pitman

Finding Daycare: Navigating the Murky World of Child Care in Today's Society by Tracy Cassels

Healing from a Homebirth Cesarean by Courtney Key Jarecki

Healing Your Attachment Wounds: How to Create Deep and Lasting Intimate Reationships by Diane Poole Heller

The Highly Sensitive Child by Elaine N. Aron, PhD

Mothers and Others: The Evolutionary Origins of Mutual Understanding by Sarah Blaffer Hrdy

Our Babies, Ourselves: How Biology and Culture Shape the Way We Parent by Meredith Small

The Positive Breastfeeding Book by Amy Brown

Raising Your Spirited Child, (3d ed. 2015) by Mary Sheedy Kurcinka

A Secure Base: Parent-Child Attachment and Healthy Human Development by John Bowlby

Sleeping With Your Baby: A Parent's Guide to Cosleeping by James McKenna

Websites

Disabled Parenting Project: www.disabledparenting.com

Evidence Based Birth: evidencebasedbirth.com

Evolutionary Parenting: evolutionaryparenting.com

Holistic Sleep Coaching: holisticsleepcoaching.com

Jack Newman on SNS Use: https://www.youtube.com /watch?v=ezGlkIkhC_o

Kelly Mom: (breastfeeding support) kellymom.com

Parenting Science: parentingscience.com

Possums Sleep Intervention: education.possumsonline.com /programs/sleep-film

NewMomHealth.com: A collaboration from the 4th Trimester Project team at the University of North Carolina at Chapel Hill Center for Maternal and Infant Health, in partnership with The American College of Obstetricians and Gynecologists (ACOG), Black Mamas Matter Alliance, Le Leche League International, March of Dimes, Postpartum Support International, and a growing list of advocacy and support organizations for postpartum mothers.

Breastfeeding and Relactation Resources

Association of Breastfeeding Mothers—Information about relactation: abm.me.uk/breastfeeding-information/relactation/

First Steps Nutrition—How to prepare formula safely: firststepsnutrition.org/making-infant-milk-safely

The Lactation Pharmacist: Facebook.com/TheLactationPharmacist

LactMed Database—Medications and breastfeeding: toxnet.nlm.nih.gov/newtoxnet/lactmed.htm

La Leche League (National and Local Chapters)

References

Brown, Amy. *Positive Breastfeeding Book: Everything You Need to Feed Your Baby with Confidence,* August 6, 2019.

Cassels, Tracy. *Finding Daycare: Navigating the Murky World of Child Care in Today's Society,* March 4, 2019.

Cassels, Tracy. "The Role of Breastfeeding in Self-Regulation." *Evolutionary Parenting*, April 13, 2019.

Eckman, Paul. *Emotions Revealed: Recognizing Faces and Feelings to Improve Communication and Emotional Life,* March 20, 2007.

Frellick, Marcia. "AMA Backs Extending Medicaid to 12 Months after Childbirth." *Medscape*, June 14, 2019.

Hunziker, Urs A., and Ronald G. Barr. "Increased Carrying Reduces Infant Crying: A Randomized Controlled Trial." *Pediatrics*, vol. 77, no. 5, May 1, 1986.

McKenna, James J., et al. "Potential Evolutionary, Neurophysiological, and Developmental Origins of Sudden Infant Death Syndrome and Inconsolable Crying (Colic): Is It About Controlling Breath?" *Family Relations*, vol. 65, no. 1, 2016, pp. 239–258.

Montagu, Ashley *Touching: The Human Significance of the Skin.* Harper Paperbacks, September 10, 1986.

Neifert, M R. "Prevention of Breastfeeding Tragedies." *Pediatric Clinics of North America*, US National Library of Medicine, Apr. 2001, www.ncbi.nlm.nih.gov/pubmed/11339153.

Nicholson, Barbara and Lysa Parker. "The Basics of Bottle Nursing." *The Attached Family*, July 14, 2009.

Sears, William & Martha. *The Attachment Parenting Book*, Little Brown Spark, August 7, 2001.

Small, Meredith M. *Our Babies, Ourselves: How Biology and Culture Shape the Way We Parent*. Anchor, May 4, 1999.

Spock, Benjamin. *Common Sense Book of Baby and Child Care,* July 14, 1946.

US Department of Health and Human Services, National Institutes of Health, National Institute of Child Health and Human Development. *The NICHD Study of Early Child Care and Youth Development,* 2006.

Index

Cosleeping, xx, xxiii, 9–10, 75–79,
    with adopted children, 79
"Crunchy" parenting, 7
Crying, 83. *See also* Sleep training
belief in the language value of,
    xx, 10–11
    importance of soothing, 89
    reasons for, 83–88

D

Doulas, 29
Dream feeding, 59
Dry nursing/suckling, 27, 45

E

Emotional regulation, 3, 88
Empathy, 3
Endorphins, 22
Excitable temperaments, 90

F

Faces, 70–71
Fathers, 44
Feminism, 15–16
Finger feeding, 58
Floor time, 100
Formula feeding, 51–52. *See also*
    Bottlenursing
    nighttime, 59
Fourth trimester, 32
Free-range parenting, 18
Frellick, Marcia, 107

G

Gellar, Pamela, 23
Gettler, Lee, 43, 44
Golden hour, 22
Gray, Peter, 44

H

Harlow, Harry, 4
Helicopter parenting, 18
Henderson, Amanda, 22
Hookway, Lyndsey, 97
Hormones, 22, 27, 35, 42–43, 44,
    50, 66
Hospital stays, 91–93. *See also*
    Neonatal intensive care unit
    (NICU)
Hrdy, Sarah Blaffer, 15
Hunger cues, 63, 86

I

Idle parenting, 18
Independence, 16
Induced lactation, 45
Infant massage, 34
International Board-Certified
    Lactation Consultants (IBCLCs),
    43, 66

K

Kangaroo care, 25–28, 53–54
Kurcinka, Mary Sheedy, 90

L

Lactation consultants, 43
Letdown sensation, 58
Lorenz, Konrad, 4
Lying-in period, 32–33

M

Male parents, 44
Maternal health, 107
McGann, Bridget, 55
McKenna, James, 43, 76

W

Wilson, Edward O., 15
Woman That Never Evolved, The
   (Hrdy), 15
Working mothers, 52

Acknowledgments

First and foremost, I want to thank Alanis Morissette for her relentless support. Alanis, you're my sister, my mentor, and my best friend. Thank you so much for being there for me in my darkest moments and loving me unconditionally. Also, thank you for educating me even further on attachment theory and providing some of these amazing resources.

Dr. Sears, you have been such a light in my life. Getting to know you and your family has been a huge blessing—the authenticity you bring to your work is so evident, and you have given me so much as a parent, and as a friend.

Martha Sears, I think of you as a second mother. The hours you spent with me making sure my words were clear was such a surreal experience. Thank you, thank you.

Hayden Sears, you have been such a friend and a sister. It has been such an honor getting to know you and feeling so supported through your words and actions these past few years.

Dr. Jay Gordon, thanks for always keeping the faith. From the moment you jumped on a plane to Ethiopia based on nothing but my word that there were children to help, I knew I'd found a kindred spirit in you. Your understanding of the breastfeeding relationship is preternatural, and I'm always learning from you!

To Bridget McCann, I never would have guessed when we met online what an incredible collaborator you would turn out to be. Your dedication to human development and anthropology is a gift to the world, and I'm so excited about the impact your research and work will have on attachment parenting.

Morgan Shanahan, you practice what you preach, girl. I am so grateful to know you and experience this entire book journey with you by my side.

To my parents, thank you for modeling attachment parenting to me before I could even speak.

Jessie, Ali, and Grammy, thank you for being such a huge support system for me....I love you so much.

And to my sons, Samuel and Aram, you have been my greatest teachers of all. Hold onto Jesus.

About the Author

Jamie Grumet is a well-recognized advocate for children's health issues globally. She has been featured on the cover of *Time* magazine, *Pathways to Family Wellness*, and *The Attached Family*, and appeared on *Nightline*, the *Today Show*, *Anderson Live*, *Dr. Drew*, and *Good Morning America*, among others.

As a writer, Jamie has contributed on attachment parenting, adoption, and children's health for HLN, *Mom*, *Kindred + Co*, *MomsLA*, *BlogHer*, and *Pathways to Family Wellness*, and was named one of the most inspiring "mom bloggers" by Mashable.

CPSIA information can be obtained
at www.ICGtesting.com
Printed in the USA
BVHW091615101119
563306BV00001B/1/P